GRIND

A Modern Guide to City Living.

Coffee, Cocktails, Recipes & Stories.

Words by Teddy Robinson
Photography by Luke Albert

Hardie Grant

QUADRILLE

Contents

In the Beginning – Shoreditch Grind

The first Grind opened its doors in Shoreditch in 2011, in a small circular building perched on Old Street roundabout in east London. In a past life, it had probably been part of an escape tunnel for the tube station, but more recently it had been a mobile phone shop owned by the Grind founder David's dad. When his father passed, David decided to call time on selling phones and turn it into the coffee shop the pair had long talked about.

The flat white hadn't really arrived in London yet, but it was about to. London was also growing up, and for the first time Shoreditch felt right in the middle of it, filling up with creative agencies and tech start-ups fuelled by coffee from Grind. Before long, Shoreditch Grind became a cocktail bar, too, led by a killer Espresso Martini.

Kaz, a DJ from Melbourne, who had helped David set up Shoreditch Grind, added a recording studio upstairs for friends and regulars to use when they were in town.

Despite all the offers and questions, it was a few years before another Grind followed. First Soho Grind, then a handful of others across London. Each bigger than the last, they became proper restaurants – burning the candle at both ends to serve coffee, food and cocktails seven days a week.

Today, we serve more than two million cups of coffee a year in our own stores, and 12 million more are made around the world by our customers at home and our friends at Soho House, using Grind coffee from our London roastery.

That's a lot of coffee.

Back in 1993, in a little round building perched on the edge of Old Street roundabout, my dad first opened the doors to his mobile phone shop, our family business.

Later, as a teenager, I worked in the shop with my dad most summers. Having started in the rag trade on the market stalls in 1980s east London, he always had an eye on the future, and although business was good, we knew it wouldn't be a phone shop forever. As we watched the world around us change, we often talked about turning the building into a café or a bar one day, somewhere people could meet up and hang out.

We loved that building – our little piece of London.

Fast-forward to 2011, and east London (and the world) had changed a lot. I was in my early twenties, and as a side project, around a job I was falling out of love with, I took over the business and turned it into a coffee bar called Shoreditch Grind. I was sick of chain coffee shops and wanted somewhere I could get a proper cup of coffee like I could in Melbourne or New York.

Sadly we didn't get to do it together, and I wish more than anything that he could have seen what we've done with the place. I know he would have loved it, and would have got such a kick knowing that something so much bigger had grown from our little round shop.

When we first opened the doors one morning in the summer of 2011, much to my surprise some people came through and bought a coffee almost straight away. Unfortunately, I missed this milestone moment as I was still upstairs finishing off the stools with a belt sander. Thankfully people liked what they saw and have been coming back ever since, because I wasn't much of a carpenter.

A lot has happened in the decade since. Thank you to everyone who's bought a coffee, a cocktail or a tin over the years. There have been a lot of ups and a few downs, but turning that little shop into a coffee bar has been the best decision I ever made. I can't wait to see what the next ten years have in store for us.

As ever, I'll see you at the Grind.

David
Founder & CEO

what is this feeling
called love?

How to Use This Book

In 2012, I got a job washing dishes at Shoreditch Grind, because I needed the money and because I really fancied one of the baristas who worked there. There were only about a dozen staff back then, and I would pick up shifts around my lectures at Central Saint Martins. It's now been about nine years since we bought a dishwasher, and I've been the creative director of Grind for almost my entire adult life.

I have no authority, academic or otherwise, to tell anyone how to live their life. I've lived on my own for my entire twenties, gone to work every day at the same company and taken fewer holidays than I probably should have. I am, however, profoundly grateful for having been able to spend the last decade with some remarkable people, including those who let me write a book with four uses of the word 'unfuckable' as an adjective.

When we first started talking to publishers, some urged us to make it a traditional recipe book and were horrified when I told them that it was going to be – at least in part – about living in London. For me, the heart of Grind has always been the everyday-ness of it all – the comings and goings of the thousands of people who have made us part of their day over the last decade. The first dates, the break-ups, the drinks with friends you've not seen in months – these are things that matter.

This book is a collection of recipes, stories and guides, written over the year spent in lockdown during the Covid-19 pandemic – a time when we've missed city living more than ever. You'll find here some of our favourite recipes from a decade of serving coffee, food and cocktails across London.

You'll also find guides to the trials and tribulations of modern city living – something for which there is no recipe. Modern London is vibrant and electric, but in a big city, the highs are very high and the lows are very low. These guides are from a time, and a place. They're from far too many overheard conversations from the queue, and abso-fucking-lutely, under no circumstances, to be taken as good advice.

Teddy Robinson
Creative Director

Mornings at Grind

We open pretty early at Grind. We start at the very beginning – it's a good place to start. Whether it's coffee for cabbies on their way home, or bacon sandwiches for those on their way to work in the City, Grind – and London – comes alive early in the morning.

Once the doors open, it doesn't take long for a queue to appear, tailing outside Shoreditch Grind and on to Old Street. It's usually builders in first, or people still out from the night before. Soon after, breakfast begins, with some of the same dishes you'll find below. We have the music up louder than it should be, and by 9am we'll have served hundreds of coffees, and smashed more than a few avocados.

Grind Guide #001
How to Make
<u>Really Good</u>
Avocado Toast

As every newspaper will tell you, avocado toast is literally the reason you haven't bought a house yet and probably never will, you loser. You see that girl from university you still follow on Instagram? She's bought a house, and it's 100 per cent because she didn't spend all her money on avocado toast.

What you might not know is that as well as being the source of all your financial woes, avocado toast is also really fucking easy to make at home. This is for two key reasons:

· Everyone can make toast.

· Avocados are a gift. It's like God looked down upon the earth after practising with the orange and the banana and was like: 'How about if this next fruit isn't just tasty, but also literally spreadable – hold my beer.' It's right there in Genesis 13:1 – look it up.

While it's easy, there are also a few tips for making really good avocado toast. Here's what you need to know.

Avocado

What restaurants don't want you to know, and will probably never admit, is that it's not just good cooking that makes their food good; the produce they have access to is out of this world.

There's an entire secret supply chain that means the fruits and vegetables restaurants use are bigger, fresher and in all ways better than the ones you buy in the supermarket. Thankfully, their suppliers also work with market traders, like Ted's Veg in Borough Market, next door to London Bridge, which is why everything there is so great too.

Of course, the other important thing to remember with avocado is ripeness. Squeezing an avocado for ripeness is everyone's go-to but, unless you're a full-time avocado fondler, you've probably not got a great point of reference – and it's a difficult one to describe. Our secret trick is using the stalk, which protrudes as a chalky little nubbin at the tip of the avocado. What you're looking for is one that you can pick off with your fingertip, to reveal a bright spot of ripe green hidden underneath. If you can't pick the stalk off, even with your fingernail, your avo isn't ripe yet. If you can, but it's brown underneath, she's probably seen better days.

Toast

Like most things in the kitchen, good toast is about doing a small number of things properly. Once, someone gifted us a toaster at Grind HQ because they thought they had invented the best toaster ever. It even had a screen. There were all sorts of strange functions, such as a button labelled 'Take a Peek!' that, when pressed, would trigger a loud whirring noise and cause your half-cooked toast to emerge from inside, pause in presentation of its untoasted-ness for you, and then recede like a carbohydrate hermit crab.

Making toast does not need to be this complicated.

Get some good bread, of whatever variety you like, give it a lick of olive oil, and put it under the grill (broiler) for a couple of minutes on each side.

Your Secret Sauce

The best part of avocado toast is that you can add almost anything: another ingredient, a garnish – or both. Sriracha is for the uninitiated. We're talking putting *anything* on it. Just looking at raw vegetables alone, the possibilities are endless. You can add fresh radishes or beetroot (beets) for incredible colours, or pea shoots for sweetness. Chickpeas (garbanzo beans) are easy as they come in a can, but you can go further – try adding kimchi or edamame beans.

Açai Bowls
with gluten-free granola

The humble açai bowl might not be as à la mode as it was in 2018, but it's still a lazy Sunday morning staple for us. Preeya – who meets and hires every member of the Grind team – insisted we put it on the menu, and it stuck. Like the best of food, you get out what you put in with açai, so we've included our recipe for homemade granola below, too. Most of the ingredients can live forever in your freezer or in the cupboard for a rainy day, and then you can throw it together in minutes. It's the perfect breakfast in bed, but go eat it in the sunshine if you can.

Serves 1
1 banana, frozen
1 mango, frozen
100g (3½oz) açai pulp, frozen
2 tbsp oat or coconut milk

For the gluten-free granola
1kg (2lb 4oz) gluten-free oats
150g (5½oz) hazelnuts
100g (3½oz) pistachios
150g (5½oz) almonds
150g (5½oz) pumpkin seeds
150g (5½oz) sunflower seeds
25g (1oz) ground cinnamon
170ml (5½fl oz) olive oil
170ml (5½fl oz) agave syrup
2 vanilla pods, seeds
    only – or ½ tsp
    vanilla essence

Garnishes: anything
    – granola, coconut flakes, chia
    seeds, goji berries, cocoa nibs,
    strawberries, blueberries,
    passion fruit, dried apricots

Slice your banana and mango and throw them into a blender with the frozen açai and milk.

Blitz until it has the consistency of sorbet.

Pour or scoop the mix into a bowl – a chilled one ideally!

Now, for the granola. Heat the oven to 160°C (320°F).

Combine everything together and mix thoroughly.

Place the mix on to a baking tray lined with greaseproof paper and bake for 25–30 minutes or until golden brown.

Once it's cool, crumble and keep in an airtight container in a cool, dry place.

Add your garnish to the açai bowl and eat.

Grind Sweet Potato Cakes
with harissa, yoghurt & eggs

This is one of our absolute favourites, and also the only dish you can find on the menu at any time of day. We serve this one from as early as 6am to as late as midnight on some days, and will likely do so for years to come. It takes a really, really good picture, and considering it's not much more complicated than beans on toast once you've prepped the cakes themselves – which you can do in advance – it looks pretty sophisticated. You've already impressed us.

Serves 3

250g (9oz) sweet potato, peeled
25g (1oz) harissa paste, plus extra
    for garnish
50g (1¾oz) plain (all-purpose) flour
    – or gluten-free flour
3 tbsp water
vegetable oil, for frying
2 medium or large eggs
2–3 tbsp yoghurt
sea salt and black pepper

Wash and grate your sweet potato like your life depends on it, on to a fresh, clean dish towel and wrap it up like a little parcel of joy.

Keeping your parcel together, squeeze tightly until the liquid drains out. Remember, you don't want to dry your sweet potato out, just remove the excess moisture.

Place your freshly squeezed sweet potato into a large mixing bowl, adding the harissa paste, flour, water, salt and pepper. Mix it together.

Once mixed, scoop out a cupped handful of the mix and shape it into round, flat patties – you'll make around six with the quantities here.

Cover the bottom of a shallow pan with oil, and heat it on the stove until it starts to sizzle. Carefully add your patties without splashing the oil, and then flip them every minute with a spatula or a fork. Meanwhile, bring a pan of water to the boil for your eggs.

As your patties start to brown, it's time to get your plate ready. Mix some harissa with a dollop of the yoghurt and add to the plate.

Break your eggs into separate ramekins. With the heat turned down a little, stir the hot water to create a little hot whirlpool and carefully pour your eggs into it one by one – we don't want to break the yolk on the rim of the ramekin being too cautious, but also don't want to 'dunk' the eggs and have them hit the bottom. Remember, keep flipping your patties!

After 3 minutes, or 4 if you prefer a firmer yolk, scoop out your eggs using a slotted spoon and let them rest on a plate lined with paper towels.

Once your patties are crispy brown, scoop them from what oil is left and add them to the plate. Assemble your patties into a stack, with your eggs on top.

Enjoy. We find you get the best photo of these if you can catch the egg right as it splits and a sunset yolk rolls down the side, but we'll leave that part to you.

Grind Guide #002
Bottomless Brunch Etiquette

We daresay we've been to more bottomless brunches than most. The Grind crew have seen it all – the lofty highs and the gut-wrenching lows, the stolen glassware, the impromptu karaoke, the friendships made, the hearts broken. If you've said it, we've heard it; if you've spewed it, we've mopped it up. It's safe to say that a lot can happen in 90 minutes. By now, we reckon we've got a pretty good idea of how to do the bottomless brunch right. Here are our tips for retaining your dignity.

Don't Be Late

At Grind, and just about everywhere else, the prosecco clock starts ticking as soon as your first bottle opens. If you're the last to arrive, hard luck – playing catch-up never ends well.

Don't Be Hungover

The only thing worse than being hungover is being hungover at a bottomless brunch. The smell of food, the look of food, the many people having a nice time, the smell of food again – it's hard to bear. Don't make plans the night before.

Move on After Two Hours

Emerging from a bottomless brunch is a bit like emerging from the cinema in the afternoon - you really don't expect it to be that bright outside. And yet it's still the middle of the day and, bafflingly, life continues soberly around your prosecco bubble. There's no cover of darkness to take the edge off, so you're left to trudge elsewhere. What you should have done was sorted out something else – it's 4pm, but let's call it an after-party anyway.

No Starving

Go as big on the brunch as you do on the bottomless. There are people who can sink two bottles of prosecco per açai bowl and then function as a human being afterwards. Assume you are not one of them. Get a full English with a side of hash browns – we are lining the stomach.

Even more importantly, don't forget to eat. You don't want to make the classic blunder of being the bottomless brunch neophyte,

and ending up fucked. They said they'd never leave you behind, but now you are alone heading wherever it is that the Northern Line takes you. You are a menace.

Be Nice to the Staff

People who are rude to staff in restaurants, bars, cafés and just about anywhere else are the lowest of the low. This is the single worst red flag on a first date and renders you nuclear-meltdown unfuckable, without question. There's really no more to say here.

Grind Guide #003
How You Like Your Eggs in the Morning

As everyone knows, the best way to enjoy eggs in the morning is with a kiss. It's been said that the kiss is so important, in fact, that the way the accompanying eggs are prepared is rendered irrelevant. Unfortunately, we're in the eggs business and not the kissing business. A tragic misstep.

That aside, the question remains: how do you like your eggs in the morning? The way someone takes their eggs can reveal a lot about them. For that reason, we advise that early into all new relationships or friendships you meet your partner for brunch. That way, you can see what they're really like, or if your eggs are just too different and it'll never work. For us, eggs are like star signs – egg-strology, if you will. They provide meaning and direction in your universe, and if you've had a really good egg, you'll understand. You stare at the menu, the menu stares back at you. The eggs see who you are, they peel back your own flaky shell and bore holes into the yolk of your soul with a Marmite soldier.

This is more than your breakfast, this is everything you are.

Boiled

Boiled eggs are sensible. They are Mark from accounting, the ready-salted crisps of people. Those in a relationship with a boiled egg can sometimes find them to be awkward and emotionally closed – they have raised this with boiled egg, who apologized, but doesn't seem to be doing anything about it. If boiled egg had a dog, it would be brown and inconsequential – the vanilla flavour of dog, default dog with factory settings. It wouldn't love them. Boiled egg thinks that Windows Vista wasn't as bad as people thought – it was a real workhorse of an operating system, if you ask them. But you didn't, did you?

Sunny-side up

Sunny-side up is gooey-centred and sentimental. Sunny-side uppers cry in every movie, even the ones that don't have dogs in them. Sunny-side uppers know what Hogwarts House they'd be in, and worse still they think you're interested to know. They want to get married at Disneyland, even though they're 36 years old. They have a cat they secretly think is much cleverer than your cat, and they like books, but not in a normal way like reading – but in a strange way where they've made liking them their whole identity. They're passionate about what they believe in, go to great lengths to fight for their cause, but are really annoying about it. Sunny-side uppers don't know irony, or cynicism, or the crushing disappointments of real life. They giggle hither and thither, and nobody should giggle hither and thither.

Easy over

Easy-over eggs are fun and carefree, they're a flexible breed. No one knows what easy-over eggs are, but they don't want to remind you because they don't want to make you uncomfortable – like the time everyone forgot it was their birthday and they took down the decorations before people asked. Easy-over's favourite sports team is your favourite sports team, but it was another one last week and you can't remember. Easy-over has worked here for ages, you think, but no one can remember how long.

Scrambled

Scrambled eggs are a hot mess. They want people to call them 'Scrammy' because they say that's what their friends from uni did – but they didn't and they made it up. Scrambled egg's phone has a cracked screen and they're just going to leave it like that. That's not something a normal person should do; that's something an animal does. Scrambled egg orders shit off the internet every day and hoards parcels around them like they're constructing an enormous Amazon box nest. Their boyfriend has one of those earrings where they've stretched their ear into a gammy flesh hoop. HR has its eye on scrambled egg.

Poached

Poached eggs think a little too much of themselves. They are smug and like the Royal Family. They are going out, but not out-out. They used to wear vintage football shirts to the office, but now they wear Stone Island. Poached eggs have friends, but their friends are all poached eggs too. They all went to private school together, but won't admit it. Poached eggs aren't as young as they used to be but are still one of the lads. They're thinking about going keto – that's just because their girlfriend is doing it; they don't even know what it is. You wonder what their girlfriend is like. Should someone tell her? She's probably a poached egg too.

One-pan Eggs

Our one-pan eggs have been on the menu in some form since the beginning. It's changed a lot, starting as a humble shakshuka, then spending some time spicy with sausages and bacon. Today, it's a lot lighter and a lot more simple, with plenty of spinach – not that you'd know it.

While the gochujang isn't essential and can easily be substituted for chilli sauce, it's a nice touch and you'll find it in a lot of our recipes – it's a sweet, spicy Korean paste made from fermented glutinous rice, but it's got a lot more character than chilli sauce. Look at us, talking about adding depth and character like this is a proper recipe book. Oh, and now we've acknowledged you, the reader. Stop! This is getting too meta!

Serves 2
vegetable oil, for frying
2 medium brown onions, sliced
1 red pepper, sliced
1 clove garlic, sliced
800g (1lb 12oz) canned chopped
   tomatoes
20g (¾oz) gochujang
50g (1¾oz) spinach
4 medium or large eggs
bread for toasting – your choice,
   we use sourdough
sea salt and black pepper

Garnish: sliced spring onion
   (scallion), chilli, coriander
   (cilantro)

In a flat pan, heat a splash of oil at medium heat and add your onions, red pepper and garlic.

We're going to sauté them, so keep them moving and turning until they begin to brown, then add the canned tomatoes, gochujang and salt and pepper.

Give the whole mix a stir, turn the heat to low and leave to cook for 45 minutes, stirring occasionally. That's a long time, especially if you're cooking with gas or don't have a lot of ventilation in your kitchen, so make sure to check on it.

Now 45 minutes older and wiser, you'll find the tomatoes will have broken down and that your whole kitchen smells amazing. You'll need to heat the grill (broiler) to medium now.

Turn the heat back up to medium, add the spinach, give it a stir, and break your eggs into the mix, then give the whole lot 3 minutes.

Now, put the whole pan under the grill to finish for 3–5 minutes. Keep an eye on it, which will probably be easy if your pan handle keeps you from closing the oven door like mine does. Oh, and put your bread in the toaster.

We're looking for the whites of the eggs to be cooked, but the yolks to be runny. When you're ready, put something down on your table or kitchen surface to rest the hot pan on and take the whole pan from the oven.

We garnish it with spring onion (scallion), sliced red chilli and coriander (cilantro), but you can add more spinach, or whatever you like really. Depending on how much you've made, this one is great served family-style with everyone helping themselves from the pan, but it's just as good for one – and that way people won't complain when you double-dip your toast.

Egg & Bacon Brioche,
chilli mayo

Years ago, we'd drive to Kempton Park Racecourse every other Tuesday for its antiques market to pick up bits and pieces for the restaurants. While the market ran all day, it's no secret among regulars that the best bits would be long gone by 8am. So, going to Kempton meant a gloomy 4am start, and a drive from east London, through the sleepy city centre, past Chiswick and out to the racecourse with a fistful of cash – you'd be laughed at for even trying to pay with a card, or asking for a receipt. It's like a Guy Ritchie movie out there. While it was a great place if you wanted a 19th-century stuffed circus bear, or a complete set of Princess Diana memorial lampshades, the best memories of Kempton were the greasy bacon sandwiches from a trailer, along with the blisteringly hot cups of builder's tea served in those polystyrene cups seen almost nowhere else since the '90s.

The antiques market still runs today, although we've not been in years. When we opened Liverpool Street Grind in 2019 and needed something on the menu that was quick, hot and probably going to kill you eventually, it was time for a reinterpretation. This is a lot boujie-er than the ones we had back in the day, but *shhhh…*

Serves 1
oil, for frying
2 medium or large eggs
2 bacon rashers
1 brioche bun, halved

For the Grind Chilli Mayo
250g (9oz) mayonnaise
50g (1¾oz) gochujang

Garnish: chopped chives

Get your pans really hot before you fry the bacon. If you're showing off, have a pan big enough, or just really hate washing up, you can probably do this in one pan, but we'd recommend two.

Break your eggs into one and drop your bacon into the other.

You want to keep your eggs moving, but let the bacon chill – not literally, mind you, it's very hot. Flip it every couple of minutes.

Before your bacon gets crispy, add your bun halves to the pan to give them a bit of toasting.

Prepare your Grind Chilli Mayo. You can't possibly fuck this up as there's only one step – just mix them together.

Once your eggs are looking soft and scrambled, pile the bottom bun half – spread with chilli mayo – with your eggs, then chives, then bacon, before topping with your top bun half.

Enjoy now, or take it with you. These are great when they're hot, and better than you'd expect when they're cold.

Grind Bloody Mary

The original and best morning-after-the-night-before drink.

Watch out though, plant people, as Worcestershire sauce is made from anchovies. You can leave it out completely or find a substitution – we use pickle juice and mustard seeds when we're making our vegan version.

Makes 1
50ml (2fl oz) vodka
200ml (7fl oz) tomato juice
25ml (1fl oz) lemon juice
Worcestershire sauce – to taste
Tabasco, sriracha, or Grind Korean
  Hot Sauce (see p74) – to taste
ice
salt, or better yet celery salt
black pepper

Glass: highball
Garnish: celery stick, lemon slice

Build the vodka, tomato juice, lemon juice, Worcestershire sauce and hot sauce in a cocktail shaker.

Add ice and shake to chill. This will only take ten seconds with a good shake.

Strain into a tall, chilled highball glass with fresh ice.

Garnish with salt, pepper and the celery stick and lemon slice, plus more hot sauce to taste. If you like, you can salt the rim of the glass.

On Wednesdays We Wear Pink

It's not like a regular drink, it's a cool drink. A layman would look at this fine concoction and tell you that it's just a gin and tonic mixed with rosé, to which we would say – so what? Clearly they've not inspected our stomach contents any time between April and October of any year, ever.

This is a summer favourite of ours, although we're certain that people just order it because of the name.

Makes 1
40ml (1½fl oz) gin
15ml (½fl oz) port
75ml (3fl oz) rosé, anything will do
50ml (2fl oz) tonic
ice

Glass: wine glass
Garnish: strawberry slices

Add the gin, port, rosé and tonic to a wine glass and give it all a good stir.

Top the glass up with ice, right up to the brim.

Slice up a strawberry to garnish. Nice and easy.

Detox on the Rocks

As both cocktails and diet plans go, this is, most definitely, without question, cheating. The Detox on the Rocks had its beginnings when we first started making our own juices, adding a big, noisy machine to the countertop and force-feeding it spinach, cucumber, apple, and whatever else green we could get our hands on. Inevitably, someone was going to try it with tequila.

Today, we make it with our Grind green juice, which we cold-press and bottle – it's a lot less messy and a lot quieter too. You can make your own green juice, or buy some – we don't mind, it's all good for you.

Makes 1
100ml (4fl oz) apple juice
1 fistful spinach or kale
½ cucumber
25ml (1fl oz) agave syrup
50ml (2fl oz) tequila
ice

Glass: highball
Garnish: celery stick or cucumber
   slices (optional)

Put your apple juice, spinach, cucumber and agave syrup in a blender, and blitz.

Pour your juice into a cocktail shaker, add the tequila and fill with ice.

Shake vigorously – we're just looking to chill it rather than dilute it.

Strain into a chilled highball glass filled with fresh ice, and garnish (if using).

Feel good about having had some of your five a day, and also tequila.

Wild Mushroom Hash

Like all the best cooking, the secret sauce here is totally overdoing it on the salt and the butter, because who wants to live forever anyway? That said, to help limit the damage, we've also included our recipe for Mushroom Ketchup. It's much nicer than anything you can get out of a bottle.

Serves 1

20g (¾oz) butter, plus extra
   for frying
150g (5½oz) wild mushrooms
   – this looks a lot in the punnet
1 clove garlic, minced
1 pinch chopped parsley
½ lemon, juiced
1 medium or large egg
pea shoots (optional)

For the hash browns

500g (1lb 2oz) potatoes – we use
   Agria potatoes, but you can use
   any medium to large potato,
   really. If it makes a good roast
   potato, it works for us.
sea salt and black pepper

For the Grind Mushroom Ketchup

400g (14oz) button mushrooms
100g (3½oz) onion, sliced
1 clove garlic, minced
butter, for frying
1½ tbsp white wine vinegar
thyme leaves
50g (1¾oz) caster (superfine) sugar
100ml (3½fl oz) double (heavy)
   cream

Garnish: pea shoots

Put your potatoes whole and unpeeled in a large pan, fill it with water and cover. Bring it to the boil on a medium heat.

Boiled potatoes go soft, as you probably know, but here we're trying to get them to al dente and no further. This should take around 5 minutes after the water has come to a boil. You can check they're done by pricking them with a knife to see if they're getting softer.

After carefully removing them from the heat, allow them to cool before peeling and grating them into a bowl.

In the meantime, heat your oven to 200°C (400°F).

Season your mix with salt and pepper, and then spread it about 2.5cm (1in) thick on a baking sheet lined with baking paper.

Bake your hash-brown mix on a high shelf in the oven for 20 minutes. Once cooked, allow to chill before slicing into pieces – we do ours in triangles about 5cm (2in) long. You can chill these in the fridge for later, or crack on!

For the Grind Mushroom Ketchup, add the mushrooms, onion and garlic to a saucepan and heat them in a little butter, keeping them moving for 4–5 minutes. Ideally, you want to do this right before the onions would go brown, but picking

your moment is a fine art here. Just wait until the onions are soft and almost translucent, then add the vinegar, thyme and caster (superfine) sugar.

Wait for the vinegar to reduce by half, then season and blitz in a blender until smooth.

Mix into the double (heavy) cream and then cover and keep in the fridge. This'll last as long as the double cream was going to, so fish the pot back out of the bin and check the label!

Heat two frying pans (skillets) with a little butter.

Fry your hash browns in one and your roughly sliced mushrooms and garlic in the other. Your mushrooms are going to reduce in size by about two thirds by the end of this.

Flip your hash browns every few minutes. You'll want to wait for your mushrooms to brown before adding in the rest of the butter and the lemon juice. At this point, break your egg into the hash brown pan.

Once your egg is done – soft or hard yolk to your preference – add your hash browns to the serving bowl, followed by all the contents of your wild mushroom pan, juices and all. Finally, top it with your fried egg and season. Garnish as you like – we use pea shoots for colour.

Grind Guide #004
An Introduction to Coffee

In his classes, one of the things that Howey, our head roaster and all-round-good-guy, likes to ask is, 'What is coffee?' Which is an odd thing to do when that's what everybody's there to learn – but that's the magic of education, I suppose.

So, what's the answer? If you ask Howey, he'll tell you that it's the seed of a fruit farmed in the coffee-growing belt in the tropics, which is picked, processed, sorted, graded, and sold, before being shipped around the world to get roasted, ground, and then turned into the cup of coffee you had this morning. If you ask someone else, they'll more likely tell you it's something that connects us, a little part of our day that we enjoy and part of the fabric of our lives. Whether you're drinking Grind coffee from a pink cup, blistering hot filter coffee in a New York Greek cup, or putting a coffee pod into a machine in your pyjamas, you're taking a moment for yourself.

At Grind, we've spent a decade serving coffee across London. We've learned a lot along the way, and we've shared it with tens of millions of people. Now you're reading a book about that journey. For us the very best part of coffee is the cup in your hands, and sharing the experience with others – but getting to that point is a long story, and it's one worth telling.

Let's start with where coffee comes from. Wrapped around the waist of the earth is what's called the coffee-growing belt, between the Tropic of Cancer and Tropic of Capricorn. Good coffee needs a few things to grow – warmth, humidity and reasonably high elevation – and that area has them in abundance. At Grind, we buy coffee from Central and South America, Africa and Mexico, but coffee also grows in India, Asia, Indonesia and the Caribbean.

Most of our coffee is grown by smallholders – farmers who own a small area of land on which they cultivate food and livestock for their own use, as well as cash crops to sell, in this case coffee. These smallholdings are family-run, and have often been farming coffee for generations – so sustainability isn't a choice for them, it's a necessity.

Coffee comes from a tree that grows up to 7.5 metres (25 feet) tall and takes three to five years to bear fruit. When it does, it sprouts rich, juicy cherries. There are a few different ways to get the seed from the cherries, but originally they were dried on beds in the sun. To do this, smallholders join together in 'cooperative societies', which share resources to operate stations that sort and prepare the coffee.

There are other methods for processing coffee, including 'washing', which involves a big spinning machine with teeth called a 'mechanical de-pulper'. There are also international variants and traditions, such as 'honey processing' in Costa Rica and 'giling basah' (wet grinding) in Indonesia, which use both the original and washing processes.

Once coffee is processed and sorted, it's graded by a handful of internationally qualified people called Q-Graders – the 'Q' stands for quality, because while very clever, they're not very imaginative. Our head roaster, Howey, is a qualified Q-Grader. This grade is – quite literally – a mark out of 100. At the top end of that scale, with grades of 90 or over, are the best coffees in the world, which are auctioned for huge amounts of money. At Grind, we only use coffee that is graded 80 or higher – that makes ours seriously speciality, as only a tiny fraction of the coffee produced internationally is graded that high.

Once the coffee makes its way across the sea, it arrives in our roastery, where it's put into our roaster, which is sort of like a washing machine mated with a rocket engine, although Howey won't like us saying that. Once roasted, the coffee is tinned by us before finding its way to our cafés – and hopefully to you, too.

Coffee History 101

Coffee has a long and colourful history, and that's just in London. Like beer, wine and bread, it's been around so long that many of the stories about its discovery and invention are closer to myth than history.

As the origin story goes, coffee first appears somewhere in Ethiopia. Given the length and complexity of making it, it's unlikely it was stumbled upon – more likely coffee back then was a different thing altogether. Looking at how vegetables have changed over the years, the coffee tree was probably pretty different too.

The first myths are set around the 13th century. There's the Sufi mystic who during his travels across Ethiopia observed 'birds of unusual vitality' and the berries they were eating. There's the Yemenite disciple who had only bitter berries to eat during his exile and tried roasting them before eventually boiling them into a broth. Sustained for days, he returned to his village – named Mocha – and was made a saint. Recorded history tells us that coffee was drunk in Yemen in the 15th century, where it had come from Ethiopia. By the 16th, it was recorded across the Middle East, Persia and Turkey, and in 1652 Pasqua Rosée opened the first coffee shop in London. You can see it today, commemorated with a plaque on St Michael's Alley off Cornhill – two minutes' walk from Bank station, and three from Grind at Royal Exchange.

The story of coffee in London and the rest of the UK is a good one. Coffee shops became eclectic meeting places for those of all classes at a time when economic and social status were more important than they have ever been – at least until the invention of Instagram, I suppose. People would give lectures in coffee shops, or run between them presenting the day's news like a town crier. They were also places for conversation about the topics of the day, where those from all walks of life could come and join in for about a penny a cup.

It's important to remember that until then people were, for the most part, frequently drunk. Thames water was polluted and rancid, and filtering methods weren't really available. People mostly drank beer or ale. Suddenly there were almost half a million people both rocket-fuelled on caffeine and – for the first time ever – sober. What follows is a whole mess of economic growth – which, for the sake of a good tale, we're going to credit entirely to coffee. The London Stock Exchange started in a coffee shop, after traders were expelled from the Royal Exchange for bad behaviour and began trading securities there. At the same time, auctioneering appeared, as did the insurance industry. While the East India Company grew across the world, it was supported in no small part by the credit, markets and securities that exploded following London's

collective hangover. Despite some bumps in the road – a plague and the Great Fire of London – the idea of coffee shops as meeting places remained largely unchanged in London for hundreds of years. While coffee fell in and out of favour, it remained a permanent fixture in a similar form up until the 20th century.

In the modern era, it's hard to imagine how coffee could be more popular, or more pervasive in our culture – at least in the west. The original coffee trend took centuries to move from monasteries in Yemen to penny cups in London, but now a viral coffee video travels the world in minutes. The big coffee companies roll out new novelty drinks on the same day in hundreds of countries, with coordinated, localized marketing campaigns and social-media strategies. Coffee isn't going away any time soon.

Grind Guide #005
Coffee at Grind

Today at Grind, we make a lot of coffee. It's roasted in our London roastery before travelling across the city to be brewed – thousands of cups of it a day.

Over time, we've developed a style of coffee of our own, based on the Melbourne flat-white culture that inspired Grind's beginnings. This mainly comes down to how we steam and pour milk. Traditionally, different coffees have different ratios of espresso and milk, but also vary in the way the milk is steamed – a cappuccino is piled with what can only be described as froth, while the original flat white has a very thin foam, and the latte is somewhere in between.

Instead, at Grind all milk drinks are served with the same silky microfoam, with each drink changing according to the proportion of milk to espresso – plus some other bits such as chocolate. As we've always said, the best coffee is the one you enjoy, and this is how we've been enjoying ours.

Flat White

The flat white is our most popular drink, and the one we're most famous for. It's synonymous with Melbourne coffee culture, but today it's drunk all over the world.

A double espresso with steamed milk, it's served in a smaller cup than a latte, and is a slightly stronger drink. We serve ours in a tulip cup.

There is a lot of debate about who created the flat white – Australia or New Zealand. We'll not get involved there, but we're grateful regardless.

40

Espresso

Espresso forms the foundation of all our coffee-based drinks. We use a double shot in every coffee as standard. The word is from Italian, meaning 'pressed out' – as the coffee is extracted through high pressure.

Some say the drink was created to cut down on the time workers were taking for coffee breaks. Like most, we serve ours in an espresso cup, also known as a demitasse.

Long Black

The name 'long black' comes from Australian café culture, where an espresso is referred to as a 'short black'. It's also known around the world as an 'americano', famously because American soldiers fighting in Italy in World War II found Italian espresso too strong, but this is probably a bit of a myth.

In the cup, a long black is a double espresso poured into a small amount of water. This offers a smoother, slightly more diluted black coffee. We serve ours in a tulip cup, the same as a flat white.

Filter

Filter coffee is the only coffee on this list that doesn't come from espresso. Instead, it's brewed over a longer time, using a larger amount of water.

In the cup, this means it is less concentrated so it's a good option if you're drinking a lot of coffee. As it's more dilute, it's a great way to enjoy the individuality of single-origin coffee. We serve ours in a tulip cup, like a flat white.

Macchiato

Macchiato comes from the Italian word for 'stained', but that's a little unflattering. This is an espresso with just a splash of milk. We serve ours in an espresso cup. As a word that sounds vaguely Italian and known as a type of coffee, its name has been pretty sullied on the high street, where you can get some pretty wild interpretations of the macchiato. For certain high-street chains, it's a huge drink covered in sugars and syrups and God-knows-what, but to each their own – no judgement. In the cup, ours is a double espresso with just a dash of milk foam.

Latte

In the cup, a latte is a double espresso with steamed milk. As it's served in a larger cup than a flat white, it has a little more milk, making it a slightly weaker coffee in terms of taste but stronger than cappuccino. Latte is short for 'caffé latte' – latte meaning milk in Italian.

We serve ours in a short glass tumbler, imaginatively called a latte glass.

Cappuccino

The cappuccino, or 'capp', is a double espresso with steamed milk, served in an even larger cup than a latte, resulting in a slightly less concentrated drink. Traditionally, it comes with a frothy head, but instead we add chocolate powder on to the espresso base before pouring the latte art in the same way as we do on our other drinks, which looks incredible. We serve ours in a mug.

The Grind Coffee Roastery, London

Before we opened the doors at Shoreditch Grind in 2011, we knew we weren't going to be happy with coffee from any of the big roasters around at the time. Much like Shoreditch itself, coffee has changed a lot in the last decade, and looking back it's hard to imagine a London without flat whites. Back then, coffee had more in common with the pitch-black, Italian-style, oily dark roast of the '90s than it does to London coffee today.

Looking for something better, we found a boutique roaster who helped us make our first Grind House Blend and roasted and delivered it to us every week. But we knew we'd want a roastery of our own soon enough.

In 2015, we crowdfunded just that. We found an old Victorian warehouse in Shoreditch, half a mile from where it all began, to host our very own Grind Roastery. We also found our head roaster in Howey, a dashing, rock-climbing biologist who also speaks Portuguese, which is useful. He's still our head roaster today, but the roastery has changed a lot since. We added a factory line to make our Grind tins, and a workshop for repairing coffee machines. We also grew out of our Shoreditch side street and into a high-tech warehouse in south London with pneumatic tubes and pink forklifts. The coffee is just as good, if not better, but Howey doesn't like that he now has to wear a lab coat.

Grind Guide #006
Drinking Coffee Like a Grown-up

Coffee is a very grown-up beverage, enjoyed by billions of teenagers across the world who've just discovered The Smiths and Bukowski and think you just, like, don't understand what they're going through. Fortunately, it's popular with other people, too.

Everyone enjoys their coffee a little differently. From the short, syrupy espressos sipped standing up in Italy, to the carefully hand-made filter coffees of Melbourne, to the flat whites we serve every day in London, it's truly international.

We've always said that the kind of coffee we make – the short flat whites that arrived in London from Australia and New Zealand a decade ago – has done a terrible job of sharing its own good news. Like many good things, this is because it has suffered from a certain kind of waistcoated, moustache-twirling, unfuckable gatekeeper who sees good coffee not as something to be shared, but as a club that is at best exclusive and at worst, elitist and sneering. At Grind, we've hated this attitude from the beginning.

For us, drinking coffee like a grown-up is about taking an interest in what you're drinking and, perhaps more importantly, sharing it with other people. Thankfully, you only need to know a few things in order to go toe-to-toe with even the most ponderous coffee snob.

Good Taste, Bad Taste
Taste is a funny one. We all have a similar amount of sensory receptors on our tongues, and we all receive the same

44

information into our brains the same way. What differs is the way we associate flavours, which depends on our background, upbringing, diet and many other factors.

The most common misconception about coffee is that bitterness and intensity are somehow linked to caffeine. Although a particularly black and bitter cup will likely wake you up in other ways, coffee's caffeine content is determined by the type of bean used – as well as by how much of it you've drunk, if that wasn't obvious.

Blends and Single Origins

In coffee, you'll often hear people talking about 'blends' and 'single origins', which are largely what they say on the tin. Blends are made using a few different coffees, while single-origin coffees contain just one. As you might imagine, blends are generally about a balance of flavour, while single origins are mostly about a coffee's individuality.

To make generalisations, coffee from Central and South America tends to be richer, sweeter, and tastes like nuts and chocolate. We use coffee from Brazil, Colombia and Guatemala as major components in our Grind House Blend for this reason. Coffees from Africa tend to be lighter, fruitier and more floral.

Brew Methods

Of course, the biggest factor affecting how coffee tastes is the way it's brewed, whether that's espresso, filter coffee, a compostable coffee pod, or even cold brew. You've likely tried most of these, given you've found your way here, but here's a quick summary:

- Espresso is a short, strong shot of coffee. It's drunk by the hardcore on its own or, more often, mixed with milk as a macchiato or with more milk as a flat white or latte. Alternatively, it's mixed with water and becomes a long black, sometimes called an americano. The espresso method wins out for intensity of flavour, and you can take it further to make an even shorter and stronger coffee – that's a ristretto.

- Coffee from a pod, such as our Grind pods for Nespresso machines, is made to be as close as possible to espresso. The pods are designed to be efficient in extracting coffee, which means fewer coffee beans required per cup and therefore less transporting of coffee around the world – which is good for the planet. While it's never going to be as good in the cup as a proper espresso brewed on a huge La Marzocco machine, it's pretty close – and it's an easy way to get consistently great coffee at home with no fuss. See p91.

- Filter coffee is a broad, catch-all term for any way of brewing coffee through filtration that isn't espresso. French press? V60? AeroPress? They're all filter coffee. See p50.

- Cold brew, in case it wasn't obvious, is brewed in cold water over a long time – usually 12 to 24 hours. Like filter coffee, cold-brew coffee highlights the origin of the coffee, which makes it popular with the connoisseurs. See p51.

Grind Guide #007
Making Coffee at Home

If you're used to drinking flat whites made by someone who sees coffee more as a lifestyle choice than just a way to make a living – we know a few of those – brewing coffee at home can seem daunting. However, there are just a handful of things you need to know to get started.

Buy Coffee You Like

This one goes without saying, or at least we'd like to hope so. A great way to start is to find a coffee you know and like, and work to recreate it at home. Know a café that does a pourover you love? Or just want to make your morning flat white at home? It's probably not nearly as hard as you think. When it comes to deciding which coffee beans to buy, try to think about the flavours you like in your coffee normally. If working out your opinion on 'notes of charred hibiscus' is a stretch, start with the easy ones – things like chocolate, nuts and fruit.

No matter what, only buy 100 per cent arabica coffee. That's the type of bean and, while there are others, it's the best and likely the only one you'll ever find served by a good coffee shop.

Follow a Recipe

Just like baking or cooking, brewing great coffee is a lot about accuracy – and following a recipe will help you achieve that. Unless you're making coffee with a pod machine or something that will measure the coffee for you, weighing things properly will get you most of the way there – and using the timer on your phone will do the rest.

Use the Good Water

We know this one sounds like bullshit, but use filtered water. Howey will tell you that you need a certain mineral composition to make the coffee taste good – and he's right – but it's also about taking care of your coffee machine. This isn't an excuse to buy plastic bottles of filtered water, mind you – get it from the tap and filter it yourself.

Making Coffee Using an Espresso Machine

The name espresso comes from how water is pressed through ground coffee under pressure. While this is quick, you may not say 'expresso'. Today, most coffee machines follow a similar pattern – a boiler heats the water, which is pumped through coffee to make espresso. Some machines also allow you to use the steam produced to heat and foam milk, too.

You'll need:

espresso machine

ground coffee

tamp (that tool with the handle, used to pack the ground coffee into the basket of your espresso machine)

milk (if using)

For the coffee:

Take the grouphandle – that's the handle part with the filter on the end – out of the machine and give it a good clean.

Add ground coffee to the filter; you want it to be full, but not overflowing.

Use the tamp inside the filter – we're looking to give the coffee an even surface, not squish it, so you can let the tamp do the work.

Carefully insert the grouphandle into the machine – most machines will need you to do this at an angle, and then pull it straight to seal it.

Put a cup or glass under the machine and press the button. We're not there with you, so we can't tell you which one, but hopefully it'll be obvious.

The shot should run dark and slow at first, gradually getting faster and lighter. On most machines, you'll want to run it for 20–25 seconds.

Once run, remove the grouphandle, bin the 'puck' of used coffee and give the filter a clean for next time.

For the milk:

If your machine has a milk frother, fill a metal milk jug with your preference of milk. If it doesn't, you can use a countertop milk frother and you don't need to worry about this part.

Tilt the jug and bring the tip of the wand just beneath the surface of the milk, and turn on the steam. As the milk increases in volume, push the wand deeper until the bubbling stops and hold until the temperature, like baby bear's porridge, is just right.

If you feel up to it, try pouring some latte art. If not, come visit us in London and we'll show you how.

Making Cafetière Coffee

Cafetière, or French press, is arguably one of the simplest methods of brewing filter coffee at home, and great for making coffee when you've people to entertain and don't want to be stuck pulling espresso shots. Because of the coarse metal filter, cafetière coffee has more body than drip filter coffee, but the real secret is getting your recipe just right.

You'll need:

a kettle – it doesn't have to be a fancy one

cafetière

digital scales

ground coffee

tablespoon

some way to tell the time: your phone timer, a watch – count if you have to

Boil the kettle.

While it's boiling, put your cafetière on the scales, set it to zero, and fill it three-quarters full with water from the tap, noting the weight of the water. Divide that weight by 16 – that's how much coffee you need. Keep a note of that number so you can skip this part next time.

Discard the water, and weigh out your required amount of coffee into the cafetière using the tablespoon.

Fill your cafetière with the now boiling water to the level you filled it earlier, and stir the brew until none of the grounds are floating. Start the timer, and allow to brew for 4 minutes.

Once done, lightly stir again before putting the lid on the cafetière and pushing down the plunger, stopping 2cm (¾in) from the bottom of the cafetière.

There's nothing more to do – it's ready to pour.

Making Filter Coffee

Drip coffee, often called filter coffee, is made by dripping water through coffee that is sat in a filter, generally made out of paper. There are so many different devices used to do this and – like so much about coffee – the preferences vary wildly around the world.

Most commonly, you'll see V60s and Chemex drippers, which are shaped like a cone. They brew a clean, balanced cup, and are popular with aficionados as they really highlight a coffee's individuality and origin. Fortunately, the method below works with almost any of them.

You'll need:
a kettle
ground coffee
digital scales
dripper – a V60, Chemex or other, plus compatible filter paper
timer
teaspoon

Boil the kettle, and weigh 16g (½oz) of medium-ground coffee.

Insert the paper filter into the dripper and pour some hot water through it over the sink. Filter paper is bleached, so we're just getting rid of any other flavours and warming up the paper.

Put your dripper over a cup, place everything – dripper, cup and all – on to the scales, add your 16g (½oz) of coffee into the paper cone, and then reset the scales to zero.

Begin a timer, and then start pouring the hot water over the coffee, slowly and carefully, until the scales show 50g (1¾oz).

Stir the wet coffee grounds with a teaspoon, making sure not to break the paper, until the timer reaches 30 seconds. Then, start pouring again in smooth circles over the coffee until you reach 256g (8oz) – that's a 'brew ratio' of 16:1.

Now you just need to wait. If you get down low – or you're very short – you'll be able to see the coffee dripping into the cup, which is very satisfying.

Once the water has all dripped through, you know what to do.

50

Making Cold Brew

Cold brew has risen in popularity with the rise of speciality coffee – particularly on the sunny shores of Australia and the USA, where it doesn't just rain the whole time.

As the name suggests, it is coffee that is brewed with cold water, which takes much longer and typically uses a higher ratio of coffee to water. This means that cold brew can be seriously strong, so approach with caution. While it's perhaps the easiest way of making coffee in bulk, it is a little bit time consuming.

You'll need:
two large containers, at least one
   of which should have a lid
ground coffee
digital scales
coffee filter paper
colander

Make sure to use only filtered water for this. We know we said it for all coffee, but for cold brew it's particularly important.

Weigh out 100g (3½oz) of coffee for every litre (35fl oz) of water you're planning to use.

Drop it in. Seriously, just put it in the water. Then, seal the lid and leave it overnight – we'd recommend a full 24 hours, but make sure it's at least 18 hours.

Now, this bit can be a little time consuming. You need to filter all of this water through the coffee filter paper, any way you can. You can get a lot of the coffee out by running it through a colander into the other container, but eventually it needs to go through the filter. We find the best way to do this is by just pouring it, a little at a time, through a cone of paper.

Once done, you've made it and we're proud of you. You can keep the cold brew in the fridge for three to four days before the flavour begins to change, and another three to four days after that before it's not good to drink. Enjoy it straight up or on the rocks.

Grind by Day

Grind by day needs no introduction, or at least we'd like to think so. We're part of the daily routine of thousands of people in London.

For us, the day at Grind is midday, through lunchtime, until the moment you step out of the office on a weekday – or until you start thinking about dinner at the weekend. On a bad day, it can feel like it lasts forever. On a good day, especially on the sofa, it can feel like forever too, but, you know, in a nice way.

Whether you're working from work, working from home, or just waiting for the sun to go down, we're here.

Grind Guide #008
How to Work from Home

Once, as I'm sure you'll remember, every blog, newspaper and laundry detergent brand decided to write a guide to working from home. It was a relevant thing to ask, but really, no one wants to hear it from the same people who wrote 1,200 words on what to wear yachting this summer.

Fortunately, we know a lot about working-not-at-the-office – just ask the literally hundreds of people who've complained on TripAdvisor about our music volume. Above all, we know that no one's interested in a mood board of mahogany desks and £600 cashmere sweatpants – we want to see dry shampoo and how we can get wine delivered. Preferably intravenously, by post if we must.

There are a few things that can make a real difference when you're working from home. Here's the sum of our worldly knowledge, sans bullshit.

Church and State

Try to separate your workspace from your not-workspace as much as possible. This isn't possible for a lot of us – communal areas often aren't up to scratch – but a lot of the benefits of doing so are subconscious, so you can trick yourself.

Find easy ways to change your surroundings so you can set work time apart. Light can be an amazing tool for this: by drawing the curtains or changing the lighting you can, with a bit of practice, condition yourself to switch in and out of work mode.

Rituals

If changing your setting isn't possible – or even if it is – try establishing little rituals to perform when you're beginning or ending work. These could be as simple as unplugging and plugging in your laptop, or getting your things out of the bag where you stowed them away the night before. These little moments mark when you're starting work, and when you're stopping work. We're also not making this up; this is, like, actual science.

<u>Try</u> to Stay Vertical

If you have room, try to work literally anywhere that isn't your bed. Even if it means sitting on the floor with your laptop. Your sleep needs just as much separation as your work does. If you're working from bed eight hours a day, you'll find your sleep quickly begins to suffer.

Take Care of Yourself

It's even easier to slip into bad habits working from home. Your diet, your exercise, your hygiene and even little things like your posture can have a big influence on how you feel day to day – but also affect your physical and mental health, especially when you're indoors for long periods of time. It's important to look after yourself.

Grind Guide #009

How to Make a <u>Killer</u> Burger at Home

We were going to write a recipe for this, but surely everyone knows how to make a burger. Besides, you don't want to make our burger – even though it is a very good one. It feels like it's been years since the burger revolution in London, but they're still everywhere. No matter how much you hear about jackfruit or kimchi or pulled banana peel as the next big thing, the real dirty secret of restaurants – Grind or anywhere else – is that almost everyone orders the burger. It's just that easy.

The good news is that it's really easy to make a burger at home – and not much more difficult to make it a really, really good one.

The Meat

Unsurprisingly, this is right at the heart of a great burger. If you haven't done it before, you should try making your own as you'll learn a lot from doing something so simple, even if it's just getting some good mincemeat (ground beef) and doing the shaping part. If you'd rather not, at least spend some of the time you save going to a local butcher to buy your burger rather than the supermarket. We shouldn't have to convince you to do this: you'll be doing good and you'll reap the rewards. It's also worth saying that a good burger is probably less meaty than you might anticipate, and you can have some fun with it. Breadcrumbs and seasoning are top of the list, but try grating an apple, skin and all, squeezing out what moisture you can, and adding it in.

Wherever you get your burger from, use your fingers to make the centre of it – think where the hole in a doughnut is – about two-thirds of the thickness of the outside edges. It'll only take a minute to do, but will stop your burger shrinking when cooked.

The Bread

Arguably the most important part of a burger – or at least the highest-risk part – is the bread or bun. Everyone can toast bread – it's best when uncomplicated, and we talked all about that on p15. But the bread is the handle of the burger, the reins of the burger chariot one might say, so you need to be careful. Burn it, and it'll be too brittle and will obviously taste terrible. Undercook it, and it'll fall apart in your hands – disaster.

When cooking with meat, we quickly toast the bun in the juices of the burger in the pan, which really adds flavour. Otherwise, just toast it quickly under the grill (broiler) – but keep an eye on it.

Cookery

Bizarrely, in the UK, restaurants aren't allowed to cook burgers anything less than medium-rare, which is honestly criminal, but rest assured we always play by the rules.

At home, however, you can go wild. You might be one of those people who just wants to leave your burger on a radiator until it returns to its original cow-in-field temperature – if so, that's your choice. Cooking a burger is really easy and can't possibly take you longer than ten minutes. Just keep flipping it as you go, making sure to keep that lovely crust you're frying up intact as you do. A minute before you're done, put your cheese on the burger while it's still in the pan, for maximum meltiness.

Squishiness

Everyone knows their squishiness preference when it comes to the patty itself – that's largely to do with how cooked it is. What's often overlooked is the squishiness balance of the burger as a whole. Medium-well with fried onions and a toasted bun? Much like my first marriage, that sounds like a dry affair. Anything plus a fried egg? That'll be quite the opposite.

Getting the balance right isn't hard, but if you've just bathed a charred hockey puck of a patty in ketchup, you've probably missed the point. It's all about the middle ground. We serve ours with fried onions but also avocado – at room temperature, mind you. Go for a rarer patty, some pickles and a mushy avocado, and it's a real two-hander – plus there's even a vegetable in it.

Grind Guide #010
Not Being so Terrible with Your Money

The poet Richard Brautigan once wrote that "money is sad shit" and, in a lot of ways, he was pretty spot-on – after all, the people who came to your university and told you to follow your passions inherited their money from their family's rare mineral refinery or diamond mine.

People have weird relationships to money. Most are neither the all-out 'spenders' or 'savers' that internet quizzes try to insist upon, but sit somewhere in the middle. Still, determining which direction you lean is a good way to start being not so terrible with your cash.

So take a long, hard look in the sobering mirror that is your bank balance, and take note. If you'd call yourself a serial saver, you don't need to read this. You already know the reason you haven't got a deposit for a house is because of all that avocado toast you used to order like a fucking idiot (see p14). You've changed your ways, and you've come to like living beneath the boot of the universe, on a diet of crushed insects and toothpaste.

But if you're anything other than that, this is for you. This is your Office of Budget Responsibility. You don't always have to be the friend who buys the first round and never says no, you know – you're a grown-up capable of making your own decisions. So let's do a little check-up to see what got us into this position.

What Are You Spending Your Money On?
This might seem simple, but money is complicated and adults – that's you, in case you were wondering – generally have a lot of things going on. Sad serial savers keep spreadsheets to track these things, and are then surprised when nobody is

impressed by this most unfuckable of habits. No one is suggesting you go that far, but there are lots of apps that can help you keep an eye on things.

What Are You Saving For?

Saving for the sake of saving is boring, pointless, and extremely difficult. There's literally no incentive – and no one ever really saves for a rainy day. Whether it's something small or big, having a clear goal in mind is the best way to stay on track.

What Are You Willing to Scrimp On?

For most of us, saving doesn't come without some kind of sacrifice. For the rest, for those who are very wealthy, please pay your taxes and set up a regular charity donation.

This is also the area where you'll receive the most bad advice. Saving a tenner a week on not buying coffee does not a mortgage deposit make – although admittedly we've got a horse in that particular race. But small changes to behaviour beget bigger ones later on.

Budget

Yeah, this one never feels very glamorous. Budgeting never appeared much in the TV shows we grew up watching, but there are lots of apps that can help you do it better. This doesn't have to be a spending budget, mind you – it could be a savings goal. But whether that's weekly, monthly or yearly, it needs to be realistic and not drain your determination if you don't meet it. This is about changing behaviour, not creating a rod for your own back, so don't be angry at yourself if you slip up and spend a little extra now and then – shit happens.

Grind Guide #011
Travelling Like a Grown-up

It doesn't matter if you live in Shoreditch or on a beach in Bali, everyone needs a holiday occasionally. When London is grey, or your shoe has fallen down the gap on the tube, or you've tracked dog shit into the house yet again, it's reassuring to look on the internet and see that someone, somewhere on a beach, has an objectively better life than you do – you fucking loser.

There are loads of places to go, and just as many ways to travel. For every 24-hour city break, there's a mountain to be climbed in the Andes. Some people live their whole lives yearning to see the wonders of the earth, and then never, ever stop trying to tell you about them. Seriously, Persephone, if east Asia gave you such a sense of spirituality and perspective, why are you so annoying about it?

So there's tip one – don't be Persephone. Tip two is to write the rest of these excellent tips down elsewhere – you don't want to be carrying this book around on your travels.

Embrace Your Budget

If you're travelling for a while, and you're not ye olde money, you're likely to be on some form of budget. Whether that's big or small, for a long trip or a short one, exceeding it doesn't pay off for you or anyone you're travelling with.

The card-holding voyageurs of Grind HQ insist to us that the memories of being sunburnt and food poisoned, losing laundry and shitting yourself are just as good as the five-star hotels and air-conditioned travel. We'll leave that call up to you, but it's certain that at some point everyone should experience the absolute chaos of the former. At the very least, it'll make a good story.

Be Adventurous

Even if you're being a real trouper for everyone at home and not planning to spin your yarns for the next two years, you should still be making some stories while you're away. Stay safe, of course, but do try to get out of your comfort zone. We don't mean any bullshit like rock climbing or bungee jumping. We're talking about making space for – this book's only moment of earnestness is coming up here – real experiences. We don't throw the word around lightly, but time spent away from home can be truly profound.

Take Pictures and Don't Put Them on Instagram

It's more than a bit depressing to be taking photos at all times, so part one is being selective. Your best travel experiences should not be enjoyed holding your iPhone. However, do take photos. Not at the photo-opportunity moments, but during the times in between – the car journeys, the trips to local supermarkets, the aimless pottering around.

Emma from Grind HQ suggests the following for your camera-roll bingo:

·   At least one person you meet.

·   Record of at least one hangover you will later suppress from your memory.

·   At least one adventurous, albeit terrible, culinary decision.

Think of it as an accidental diary – because we know you're never going to keep a real one, despite your best intentions. Your phone knows everything about you, and your camera roll is basically a free, perhaps less flattering, extension of your memory – so you might as well embrace it.

Grind Guide #012
Packing for Your Travels

If there's a skill all grown-ups should master – besides cooking or picking good wine or being more decisive when browsing Netflix – it's how to pack for a holiday. It doesn't matter if you've never owned a passport or if you spend more hours at 30,000 feet than at sea-level most years, there are few sins greater than wasting 15 minutes unpacking your bag in airport security because you've left something vitally important at the bottom of it. As the queue behind you tails off into the distance, a thousand pairs of eyes bore a hole into the back of your poorly organized skull – everybody hates you.

If we (a book) were to ask one thing of you (a person), it would be this: why do people pack four pairs of underwear for a one-night stay? We'd like to hope you have a 100 per cent success rate on not shitting yourself from the age of about 2 upwards, so what makes you think incontinence is going to strike this particular weekend at Soho Farmhouse? You need to reconsider.

Whether you'll be travelling out of a backpack for six months or doing a city break with hand-luggage only, we've got you covered. Essential to the art of packing is understanding that it goes far beyond what you put in your bags; it reaches to the very core of your being. Travelling through an airport is a game to be played, and here's how we play it.

Pick Pockets

To reiterate: the tendrils of excellent packing extend far beyond the suitcase. This especially applies at the airport, where all your important things will be on your person – unless you're travelling without pockets. If you have decided to travel without pockets, put this book down.

Just put it down. Put it down, go outside and think about the consequences of your actions.

If you're at all anxious when travelling, you'll want to know where your important things are at all times. The best way to do this is to consciously decide where certain things are kept. Inside pockets are great for this. For example, put your passport in your inside jacket pocket and then, when you take it out and use it, put it back in that pocket – rather than just absent-mindedly stuffing it wherever you fancy. This will save you valuable seconds of terrified full-body-self-groping every time you feel you've forgotten something. Better yet, it will prevent it completely.

Make Lists

Lists are very useful, and if you've got this far in the book, you've probably realized we have somewhat of a penchant for them. They're pretty good for most things in life, but they're particularly key to packing success. Not only are they useful for remembering what to pack, but they're also handy for holding yourself to account over the ridiculous nonsense you've chosen to include. Be bold, reader, this is the weekend you will break your shitting-yourself streak.

Take Your Time

Real talk, this one's legit advice. Don't attempt to pack everything 15 minutes before you leave. We shouldn't have to tell you this.

Packing well is a fine art and as Las Ketchup will tell you, a masterpiece takes time. If you're anything like us, that list you wrote earlier is going to get a pretty artistic interpretation once your suitcase is ready

and open, so don't pretend you can do it on the fly because you thought about it beforehand.

Travel in Style

See above on the whole pockets thing – under no circumstances travel without them unless you've got someone to carry your luggage, and your Instagram-husband-slash-human-camera-tripod doesn't count. Every item you can carry on your person means more space in your suitcase. Now, we're not suggesting you wear everything you own, because you'll be a calamity in security, and all that leather and latex will chafe. But you should definitely wear anything you're taking that could be described as 'chunky', as long as it's comfortable. If you're only going for a day, you don't need three outfits – so just wear one to travel.

Save Space

Ideally, don't pack anything you could easily buy when you get to where you're going. We don't mean everything – bring your clothes and as much as you can to reduce waste. But be conscious of what will be provided for you. Your hotel will absolutely provide towels and some limited toiletries, but you'll want to bring your own skincare.

If all else fails, just put everything in your case, sit on top of it, and pray to the packing gods that the zip won't break. Bon voyage.

Grind Guide #013
Meeting for Coffee

Networking is total bullshit. The idea that you should be networking for its own sake is deeply distressing. The suggestion of an event specifically for networking is a bit like an event specifically for making friends – anyone worth meeting won't be there.

Sadly, universities seem to be completely unaware of this, and they'll waste about a month a year telling you to go spend your student loan on business cards as if moo.com has them on commission. It's 2021, and I can't remember the last time I saw a business card that wasn't part of an American Psycho Halloween costume, or belonged to some sort of furniture salesman who was older than God. New stationery is like a new job title – a consolation prize when you ask for a raise and it doesn't work out.

Unfortunately for the printing industry, but fortunately for Grind, coffee is a good way to meet professionally, whether it's for the first time, or just the first time in a while. Models have always had the go-see, now everyone else has meeting for coffee. Here's how to make it work for you.

Emails, Unlike Revenge, Are Not Best Served Cold

This is a big one. Unless you absolutely can't avoid it, try not to email anyone cold. It might mean calling in a huge favour, or getting really creative about the degrees of separation between you and the girl your brother dated in school, but there isn't anything worse than a blind email out of the blue. If going in cold is really the only option – and our toes are curling at the thought – make sure to do your homework. For anyone who's worth meeting, their time is going to be a big deal to them, and showing respect for that is your big ticket. Your email should be brief, but every word should remind

them how much you want to meet them –
and if anything about their professional life is
on the internet, there's no excuse for not
knowing it.

Be Upfront About What You Want

Just as if you were taking their daughter to
the prom in a '90s high-school movie, you
need to make your intentions clear. Is the
person doing something you'd like to do
yourself one day, and do you want them as a
mentor? Do you want a job and feel you have
something to offer? Are you looking for
feedback on an idea? Making it clear what
you're after – and why it's them specifically
you'd like to ask – is just polite.

Meeting for Coffee is a Lot Like Going on a Date

And a lot of the same rules apply (we'll save
those for p80). 'Be yourself' might be a
cliché, and it isn't bad advice, but it's better
to be the best version of yourself. If you've
made the invitation, you're hosting – pick
somewhere that you know is convenient for
them. Make sure it's somewhere you've been
before, and if you're meeting your favourite
influencer or the creative director of your
favourite brand, we're hoping you can do
better than Pret. Oh, and make sure you're
there first.

First Impressions Are Important

But not in the way people think – it's often
a lot less about how you look and more
about the way you make people feel. Most
people love to talk about themselves, and
it makes them feel comfortable.

Win the Room

Remember, this isn't a smash-and-grab for
insights – all the long-term value here is not
in what they know, but in that they now know
you. So, needless to say, priority number one
is just making sure they don't think you're an
asshole. Seriously, it's surprising how often
this is forgotten. Last of all, as much as this
might contrast with the next point, try not to
be too mercenary. If they leave with your
résumé stapled to their forehead, this isn't
going to go well for you.

Make Your Point

You've invited them, but you're on their time,
and you should be respectful of that. A big
part of that comes with what you ask. You're
hosting, and you should probably be ready to
lead the conversation – after all, they've
agreed to meet you. As you have ideally
made sure they already know what you're
after, you can press them on the questions
that really matter. They might be your new
BFF, or at least you might think so, but even if
you're getting on, they've probably got places
to be – so don't waste their time.

The Ps and Qs

Obviously, follow up and say thank you.
You're not a barbarian.

Fried Chicken Sandwich,
Korean hot sauce, slaw, pickles

You can eat this every night – we already do.

Serves 1

For the chicken sandwich
1 boneless, skinless chicken thigh
25ml (1fl oz) buttermilk
60g (2¼oz) gluten-free flour
vegetable oil, for deep frying
1 burger bun
1 tsp mayonnaise
1 pickle, sliced
sea salt and black pepper

For the Grind Slaw
150g (5½oz) white cabbage, shredded
1 red onion, thinly sliced
1 pinch chopped coriander (cilantro)
1 pinch chopped chives
2 spring onions (scallions), finely sliced
1 jalapeño, sliced
½ lemon, juiced
3 tbsp olive oil
1½ tbsp vinegar
1 tbsp mustard
1 pinch sugar

For the Grind Korean Hot Sauce
50g (1¾oz) sugar
100g (3½oz) gochujang
½ lemon, juiced
1 tsp salt
¾ tbsp water
½ tsp fish sauce
50g (1¾oz) butter

You really can't possibly fuck up the Grind Slaw – just mix everything together in a bowl, add a little seasoning, and keep it in the fridge. Covered, mind you!

For the hot sauce, heat a saucepan on a medium heat and sprinkle the sugar evenly across the bottom. Once it browns and begins to caramelize, carefully – the sugar will be really hot now – add the gochujang, lemon juice, salt, water and fish sauce and whisk until combined.

With the pan still on the heat, whisk in the butter. You're looking to get it to emulsify – that is, mix it together until it's consistent.

Remove the mixture from the heat, leave to cool and then chill in the fridge. You can keep it in a leftover ketchup or sriracha bottle for convenience, but any sealed container will do. It'll last for about 2 weeks in the fridge.

Coat your chicken thigh with an even coat of buttermilk, and then an even-evener coat of flour, then season. Oh, and get the grill (broiler) on at a medium heat for toasting your bun and preheat your deep fryer.

Deep fry at 160°C (320°F) for 6 minutes until you get a nice golden-brown colour. It's not going to go full fried-chicken-shop

brown, but that's probably a good thing. If you've not got a deep fryer, you can do this with a pan of oil, but be careful – seriously.

While you leave your chicken on some paper towels or baking paper to rest, cut your bun in half, put the halves under the grill and lightly toast them. This should only be for about 3 minutes as we don't want them to go too crispy.

Mix a little of your Korean Hot Sauce with mayonnaise, then slather it on to your bun halves. Add in your chicken and slaw, plus the pickle and more hot sauce to taste.

Grind Guide #014
Killing It at
Your Internship

Internships are the devil. Like big brands asking creatives to work for free in exchange for 'exposure', they're pretty morally bankrupt as far as we're concerned. That said, they seem to be part of modern life and probably will be for the foreseeable future. Like it or not, when you're 21 and fresh out of university, the options are basically a graduate scheme, good old-fashioned nepotism, or an internship. The Deloitte graduate scheme is probably a pretty safe bet, but that sounds a lot like being made into ketchup – and you'd much rather be an organic grown-on-the-vine tomato, wouldn't you? Meanwhile, mumbling about how your uncle is editor-in-chief is sure to take the shine off your job on a date. So, what choice do you have?

Fortunately, you have several decades of movies and TV shows about following your dream in the big city to help you romanticize your life, while you figure out how to get through what will hopefully be just a year. We've no doubt your first taste of working life will turn out better than Anne Hathaway's, mainly because your boyfriend isn't such a piece of shit. And though we can't promise you Stan Tucci, we can offer our tips for killing it regardless. So, you've got your dream opportunity alphabetizing insurance forms in, like, the hottest insurance form alphabetization start-up right now, let's figure out how not to waste it. Ground-breaking.

Be Persistent

Wherever you'd like to intern, whether it's Goldman Sachs or your local bookshop, they won't know who you are and have already forgotten you. Before, during and almost immediately after your internship. Life is busy, and people are self-interested, so it's on you to make it happen. Send that follow-up email – what's really the worst that could happen? You will be forgotten about on multiple occasions, left to your own devices, not told what time to arrive at the office,

not told where the office is – but once
you're in the room, people will always,
mostly, occasionally, sometimes be glad
for your help.

Be Interested

You'd think this would be more obvious to
people, but you'd be mistaken. So often
when you're trying to write the perfect email
highlighting what a 'hard-working and
conscientious individual' you are, it's easy
to forget about the person receiving it
– especially when you've got a head full of
bad career advice about how every business
scans CVs for the words 'team-player' and
bins the rest. The people you want to
impress are human, and can't help but feel
good when people want to know about them,
so dropping in a question and exercising
a little flattery goes a long way.

Be Early

Whether it's for your first day, for a meeting
or a lunch catch-up – get there on time, if
not early. People often think it goes
unnoticed if you're two minutes late. It
doesn't, and people will make assumptions
about you that we know aren't true, because
we know you and we think you're great. Just
look at your taste in literature!

Ask Questions

Big or small, they all matter. The fear of
sounding stupid or uneducated can be
all-consuming, especially when you're
super-conscious of being a small fish in a
very venti pond. You're there to learn and,
trust us, no one is going to teach you, so it's
up to you.

Get Coffee

If Anne Hathaway can do it, so can you. If
there's one bit of advice to take away, it's
'be indispensable', even if you're just the
indispensable coffee-getter to begin with.

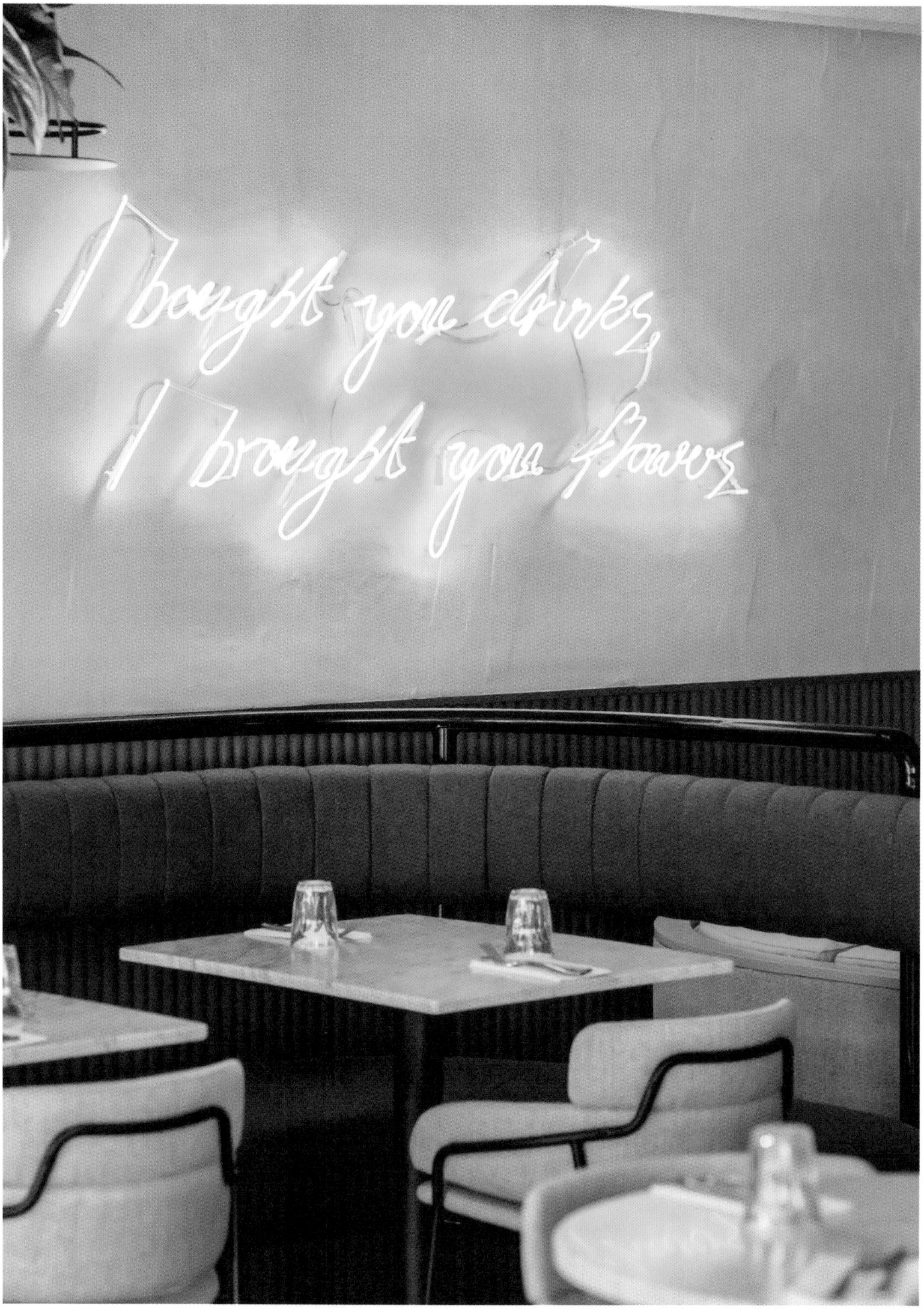
I bought you drinks,
I brought you flowers

Grind Guide #015
The First Date

You've got yourself a date, but of course you did – look at you, you're a catch.

All the hours you spent painstakingly making sure your dating profile represents a highly flattering, while totally accurate, version of the real you were all worth it. Sure, what you've written is a collage of parts stolen from other profiles, and your camera roll runneth over with eerily identical photos of you half-laughing while holding a glass of wine, but now the whole world knows you're cultured and cool but, like, in an approachable way. Like we said, all worth it. For those lucky star-cross'd few of you who've got yourself a date not through an app – we're imagining eyes locking across the tube carriage or through bookcases in a library – then we hate you. A plague on both your houses.

Incidentally, writing this has given us serious second-hand anxiety. If you read it and then go on a date, can you just drop us a message on Instagram or something to let us know it went okay? Please?

Location

According to the serial daters in Grind HQ, picking the location for your first date is 70 per cent of everything going right. To us, that seems like an oddly specific number, but we're going to go with their answer on this regardless. Whether you're picking the spot, or they are, you'll likely want to find somewhere that works for both of you – unless you have the search radius on your dating apps set seriously small and you've matched with someone on your road (which is kind of creepy but also pretty convenient). Either way, best not to be taking three tubes back to yours – or back to theirs.

No Activities

Activities are fucking garbage, so do not take anyone axe-throwing or allow yourself to be taken axe-throwing. At best, activities are someone's poor attempt to say something about themselves – there's a very particularly unfuckable type of guy who loves taking you, man or woman, to an art gallery on a first date and explaining the art to you. At worst they're a poor attempt to have something to do. You can just go for drinks or for dinner, you know – and everyone likes those. We're not biased but somewhere like Shoreditch Grind is the perfect spot for first-date drinks. Okay, that unbiased bit was a lie, but we really, really are.

Butterflies

Being a 'serial dater' is a bit of a strange idea. While it does mean you have some experience, it also implies you're not very good at it – or maybe just picky. If you're not so experienced, you'll probably be a little nervous before your date – but let's call it excitement. Whatever you're looking for from your date, it's a pretty good sign if you're nervous excited before meeting them – at any rate it shows you've not given up on life just yet. Just remember it's likely the person you're meeting is feeling a little nervous excited, too. Like your creepy neighbour said when he made you hold his tarantula: 'It's more afraid of you than you are of it.' Unlike your creepy neighbour, and tarantula, however, your date can't smell fear.

The Date

Grind HQ has spoken, and the verdict is that – wait for it, because it's ground-breaking – you should 'be yourself', just like your mum says. Being more realistic, a little polish never hurt anyone – if you scratch the faces off dolls and repaint them in your spare time, that's maybe not first-date conversation material. But equally now is not the time to be pretending you're into a band that you've never even heard of.

The Follow-up

So now comes the real mindfuck. To be completely honest, the only thing to do here is not overthink it. Yes, there's an argument for playing it cool, but if you leave it too long before letting them know you had a great time, they might start thinking the opposite. People will tell you there is a fine balance to this. There isn't. If you want to message them later that night or first thing the next day, you're welcome to – it's more about the dynamic between you than any rulebook. That being said, a little hard-to-get never hurt anyone.

Remember, there's always the chance things didn't go quite so well and that's fine too. We're big believers in giving everyone a second chance, but if you know they're just not right for you, then literally don't even bother replying, just ghost, ghost, ghost away. We're joking. No ghosting.

Burnt Cauliflower,
lime, tofu aioli

This is the plant-based meal that'll convert every carnivore you'll ever meet. Seriously, it's one of the best things you'll ever put in your mouth. Normally we're far from fans of cauliflower – it's like the Moaning Myrtle of vegetables – but we could eat this every day. Perhaps more than any other dish on the menu, it's also truly international – we've had versions that lean into the tofu with a more Asian spin, and versions with spices and pomegranate that feel almost Middle Eastern.

It's great for cooking for a lot of people too, as you can make it in minutes and the only real limit is how much cauliflower you can fit in your oven. So invite some friends!

Serves 2

For the cauliflower
1 whole cauliflower
vegetable oil, for frying
15g (½oz) coriander (cilantro), chopped, plus extra leaves, to serve
1 tbsp olive oil
1 lime, sliced, to serve
1 pinch sumac, for sprinkling

For the tofu aioli
300g (10½oz) silken tofu
1 clove garlic, crushed
1 lemon, juiced
½ tsp turmeric powder
1 pinch salt
150ml (5½fl oz) vegetable oil

Heat the oven to 220°C (425°F).

Find a pot with a lid that's big enough to contain your cauliflower whole, place it inside and fill with 5cm (2in) of water.

Put the lid on and place the pot on a medium heat for about 7 minutes to steam and tenderize your cauliflower.

Cover the bottom of a shallow ovenproof pan with oil, and heat it on the stove until it almost starts to smoke.

Cut your now-quite-tender cauliflower in half and place it into your pan. As soon as it hits the hot pan, put the whole pan into the oven. You're going to leave it to char, turning it as it does so. You're looking for proper burning here:

your halves should go dark brown, almost black in places. Surprisingly, this'll only take 10 minutes or so – turn your halves over halfway through.

Remove the cauliflower from the oven and place it on some paper towels or baking paper to cool off. In the meantime, make your aioli by throwing your tofu, garlic, lemon juice, turmeric, salt and oil into a blender and blitzing until smooth.

Toss your cooled cauliflower in a bowl with your chopped coriander (cilantro) and olive oil – you're looking to give it a proper coating.

Serve plated up with the tofu aioli, some coriander leaves, a squeeze of lime and sprinkle over a little sumac for colour.

Mushroom Lasagne

It's fair to say that this isn't our usual kind of food. This is proper wintertime, family-style eating, which we love, but sadly isn't that popular when it comes to dates, or brunch, or drinking cocktails. Still, it makes a great hungover Sunday lunch – the kind of thing you fill up on before passing out on the sofa watching Netflix. This is sleepy food.

Serves 4

butter, for frying
2 medium brown onions, sliced
2 cloves garlic, sliced
300g (10½oz) shiitake mushrooms, sliced
4 x 400g (14oz) cans chopped tomatoes
450g (1lb) fresh lasagne sheets (see p87)
120g (4¼oz) Parmesan, grated
200g (7oz) scamorza, sliced
100g (3½oz) mozzarella, sliced
sea salt and black pepper

For the béchamel sauce
100g (3½oz) butter
100g (3½oz) plain (all-purpose) flour
800ml (28fl oz) whole milk

Heat a frying pan (skillet) and a large saucepan both with a little butter, then add your onions and garlic to the saucepan.

Add your mushrooms to the frying pan, and keep them moving.

You need to sauté everything in both pans. Keep turning them as they brown, before adding the tomatoes to the saucepan with the onions and garlic. This is a good time to season, too.

Once the mushrooms have browned and softened, remove the frying pan from the heat and leave them to cool while you do the rest.

Give the whole tomato and onion sauce mix a stir, turn the heat to low and then leave to cook for 45 minutes – checking every now and again to make sure nothing's caught fire.

For the béchamel sauce, melt the butter in a small saucepan over a medium heat, then stir in the flour – our chefs call this forming a roux. Yeah, like 'Dancing on My Own'. Don't be ridiculous, obviously we know that was by Robyn. Slowly add the milk, stirring as you go to avoid lumps.

Drop the heat of the béchamel to low, and then leave to cook for 20 minutes. Give it a stir every

few minutes to make sure it doesn't stick.

Once done, leave the tomato and onion sauce to cool, or even chill if you're going to do the rest later.

Now, the lasagne part. No one really tells you this but lasagne is mainly just an assembly job. It's basically a hot savoury trifle, but it doesn't sound very appetizing when you put it like that. What this means is that you can style it largely as you want – just build layers of your various components into a suitably sized baking tray.

This is a good time to get the oven heated up – to 190°C (375°F).

Start with the tomato sauce and then the lasagne sheets, repeating layers of those two and the mushrooms all the way up. Then add more layers of the béchamel and cheeses towards the top. Make sure you top it with the cheese, though – everyone knows that's the best bit.

Finally, bake the whole lot in the oven for 25–30 minutes, or until golden brown on top. Garnish is best left pretty unfussy, so cracked black pepper and sea salt is more than enough.

Grind Guide #016
How to Make Pasta

Pasta is good for the soul. Or at least that's what your nonna would say, if you had a nonna – but you don't. In reality, pasta was invented in 1955 as a ploy to market the popular animated movie *Lady and the Tramp*. Today, pasta is just about everywhere in London – and London is surprisingly good at it given that we butcher just about every other world cuisine. Fortunately, due to a fun throwback of an idea called the European Union, London hospitality boasts incredible people from across Europe to keep our bullshit in check.

Making your own pasta isn't as hard as you probably think it is and – fortunately – everyone else thinks the same as you. That means having made your own pasta, or posting about making it on Instagram, is minimal energy for maximum reward as long as the pasta you're making isn't too laborious. However you make it, we can tell you with no certainty whatsoever that it'll taste amazing. If you invite us over, you can ask us if we like it and we'll nod and smile and clap and tell you 'well done, it's delicious' because that's just who we are – scoundrels.

Making your own pasta kind of comes in two parts: making the dough and then making it into pasta. The good thing is that it's a little flexible on timings, so you can keep the dough in the fridge for a day if you need to, and then you can refrigerate the pasta itself for a further two days, or freeze it for up to two weeks. This makes setting out to make it a bit less of a commitment, which we like.

For the pasta

220g (7¾oz) '00' flour – this 'doppio zero' flour is super fine; you can get it in bigger supermarkets

80g (2¾oz) semolina flour

12 egg yolks – hold on to the whites and make something with them later

1 tbsp water

1 tbsp olive oil

Mix the flours together in a bowl before adding the egg yolks, water and olive oil.

After a bit of stirring, the dough will come together to form a ball.

At this point you'll need to roll up your sleeves and do the work yourself – give it 5 minutes of proper kneading. The dough needs to be elastic, but not sticky.

Once done, wrap the ball in clingfilm (plastic wrap) or foil to keep the moisture in and let it rest for at least 30 minutes before rolling it out.

Rolling out your pasta into shapes is where it can get a little labour intensive if you're doing some of the fiddlier ones. Lasagne pasta is the easiest pasta to make at home, as there's no fussy pasta maker and no fiddly shapes to do – it's just dough, rolled flat. It's a great way to start making your own pasta before attempting something more complicated.

We'd recommend leaving the cute little bows and the alphabetti spaghetti to the professionals and/or robot overlords who make them. Thankfully, with or without a pasta-rolling contraption, there are easier ways to do it.

Most of these start with rolling a portion of your dough out on a cutting board. We'll do tagliatelle today as it's one people are familiar with and is super quick. Keep the board dusted with flour to prevent sticking as you roll. Your dough should be around 1–2mm (½2–¹⁄₁₆in) thick – thin enough so you can see your hand through it when you hold it up, although be careful there. If you're making finer pastas, you'll want to keep dusting them with flour to stop everything sticking together. Using a sharp knife, cut your pasta into strips. Repeat with the rest of the dough.

As you go, put your pasta to dry on a floured surface or a drying rack. If you're the kind of cat who's got a pasta-drying rack already, you should really be reading a more advanced guide. The rest of us can just use a cooling rack propped up on some books. Just don't use this one – it's special.

Courgette Spaghetti
with turmeric coconut cream and sugar snap peas

It's a shame that spiralizers became such a fad because they're a good way to eat so many things. Instagram influencers just ruin everything. Way, way back when we opened London Bridge Grind, we had a spiralled root vegetable salad on the menu that was basically all we ate for a whole summer. We don't think it was even dressed, short of a little bit of citrus, but it was so bright and summery, even though it was made up of pretty traditional winter vegetables.

This courgette (zucchini) spaghetti is a little more substantial than a salad, but it's still all plant-based goodness. While you do have to use a blender, it's also a quick-fix weeknight dinner that you can put together for one person or for six in minutes, and it feels a lot more sophisticated than a simple salad.

Serves 1

vegetable oil, for frying
70g (2½oz) shallots, sliced
1 pinch turmeric powder
230ml (7¾fl oz) coconut milk
50g (1¾oz) Tenderstem broccoli
1 handful spinach, thinly sliced
1 handful sugar snap peas, thinly sliced
120g (4¼oz) green courgette (zucchini), spiralized
sea salt and black pepper

Garnishes: sliced red chilli, crispy fried onions, black sesame seeds, coriander (cilantro) leaves

Heat a splash of oil in a saucepan over a medium heat, then add the shallots. You're looking to sauté them, so keep them moving until they soften.

Add the turmeric and keep stirring for 2 minutes before adding the coconut milk.

Let the mix simmer for another 2 minutes, adjusting the heat as you need. Don't let it boil, as we don't want any liquid to evaporate.

To make the coconut cream, pour the coconut mixture into a blender and pulse until smooth, starting on the lowest setting if your mixture is still hot.

Clean out your pan, heat a drizzle of oil over a medium heat, season your broccoli, spinach and sugar snap peas, and fry for 2 minutes.

Add the spiralized courgette (zucchini) to the pan and cook until it softens. We're looking for al dente here, but the courgette will go soggy if it gets too soft, so keep an eye on it.

Add your spiced coconut cream to a bowl, and then heap on your courgette mix before garnishing. We like to add crispy fried onions, sliced chilli, black sesame seeds and coriander (cilantro), but go wild.

Grind Guide #017
Shopping Small in London

Like everyone does, Grind started small. The arrival of the flat white in London took place in hundreds of cafés across the city, but it was driven by the support of millions of people who chose to reroute their walk to work one day, and then kept going back. It also helped that it tasted really good, and wasn't just a litre of hot milkshake.

Today, more than ever, London's independent businesses need your support. And that's not just cafés and restaurants, but independent makers and designers and barbers and everyone else who keeps the city's wheels turning. What's more, supporting small businesses doesn't mean changing your whole world. There's no expectation that you'll never set foot in a supermarket again or have to start making your own toothpaste, but there are a few key things to bear in mind to make sure your money goes to the right places.

Adjust (Some of) Your Expectations

If you're like us and you live in a major city, you've probably ordered some necessary-although-not-urgent item of stationery from Amazon and received it in a way that can only be described as blisteringly fast. We're talking like, I-needed-Sellotape-at-10am-and-now-it's-in-my-hand-at-2pm fast. While convenient, Amazon and other companies – we're looking at you, fast fashion – have changed the game in terms of what you expect from the companies and people you buy things from. This race to be the fastest, cheapest and most convenient, even when it's not necessary, is only made possible by these companies' deep pockets. Worse still, we're not talking about the raw cash they have on hand, but rather their ability to lose money – sometimes indefinitely – to give you this service.

Start Shopping Early

You might not believe it if you've sunk as many hours as we have into a YouTube hole of 3D-printing videos and people scratching off and repainting the faces of dolls, but making really great things – that aren't coffee – takes time. Independent brands and makers, especially those selling expensive items such as jewellery, might not have the funds to keep vast hoards of stock on hand like the bigger brands do, so they could need you to be a little patient, or they may even have to make items to order for you. If you take a step back from the mindset we're used to having in 2021, that's actually a nice thing.

Cut Out Fast Fashion, Completely

Yeah, we did say it wasn't like you'd never set foot in a supermarket again, but this one really needs a right-angle turn from just about everyone. Making items of clothing as cheaply as the fast-fashion firms do comes at an enormous environmental and human cost. Say it with us: the reason clothes often aren't made in the UK isn't because we don't know

how to sew, it's because labour laws and pollution regulations are more relaxed elsewhere. In a nutshell, if they were making them in the same way over here, it would be illegal. On top of this, we'd argue that fast fashion is pretty bad for you, the buyer, too. Expecting to be able to get a dress through your letterbox the same day you ordered it, and for less than a tenner, is the kind of behaviour reserved for the bad children in *Charlie and the Chocolate Factory*.

Ask Questions

This one is perhaps the most fundamental, and one we know well from our own business. When we first launched our compostable coffee pods for Nespresso machines as a sustainable way to make coffee at home, people wanted to know all the details – like how the pods were made, how they'd compost, and if we thought they were a more sustainable way to make coffee than the old-fashioned one. Having worked hard on the pods, it was great to see people taking such a conscious role in what they were buying.

There's a lot to be learned from this attitude when shopping for just about anything. As always, be conscious of greenwashing and don't hold back when you're digging into people's sustainability practices. As with most things, if it sounds too good to be true, it probably is.

Grind Guide #018

Why Your Housemates Suck (and How to Find Ones Who Suck Less)

Your housemates – and we say this with love and respect – probably suck. They suck because you found them on a website where people who suck go to find people like you. You don't know them and you're not interested in getting to know them – they're merely your counterparts on the bunk bed that is your life in London.

The only reason you're living together is because your last flatmate, whom you hated, moved in with her boyfriend, whom you hated more. She told you on Boxing Day, and gave you until New Year's to find someone. Happy fucking Christmas to you too, Katie.

Still, very occasionally, you and the people you call your friends just so happen to be looking at the same time, and you manage to find a house converted into flats that's just about nice enough, isn't in the middle of nowhere, and doesn't need you to sign over the soul of your firstborn for a deposit. And then yet, still, your housemates suck.

If hell is other people, living with them is surely its lowest, most depraved circle. Perhaps it's the ever-present-yet-somehow-never-dressed boyfriend, or the guy apparently operating a revolving door of Hinge dates? Maybe it's the one housemate who's so silent and non-present that she's not so much living in the house as haunting it. Here's how to get yourself some housemates who suck less...

Communication Is Terrible

Sorry, part of this one's on you. Your housemates suck because you probably haven't established any ground rules together, or you have but people haven't kept to them. You might be one of those people with a Notes app full of drafted rants at them written while a) drunk, b) fuming, or c) both.

Or – worse still – you might have actually sent them.

Communication is important, but somehow even the most outgoing are rendered useless when dealing with the people they live with. Whatever you do, please don't be passive-aggressive. Just because you put 'haha' and a smiley face at the end of a message and start every sentence with 'I just think that…', it doesn't mean you're being any friendlier or more constructive.

There Is Shit Everywhere

Let it be known, if you don't know who the messy housemate is, it is you. Of course, 'messy' embraces a wide spectrum of misbehaviour, but sometimes it's the smallest things that cut the deepest. Throw a party Friday and the house is a mess the next day? That's very forgivable in our book. But if there's shit everywhere, cigarette butts and unfamiliar bodies lying around on Monday, you have a problem. Do just check they're breathing though. Of course, a murderous housemate is still preferable to one who finishes the milk and leaves the empty bottle in the fridge. That's sub-human.

The Floordrobe

Closely related to the shit everywhere situation is the mysterious case of people who don't seem to have any form of storage other than where they last left things. Call it a 'floordrobe' if you will, but it also extends to never putting plates away and – perhaps most commonly – storing your clothes on the rack that aired them. Look, we're all about calling-in, not calling-out here, but men, we're looking at you on that last one.

They're Really Boring

Then there's the mind-numbing horror of housemates who might be lovely but are just so incredibly boring. You share the same four walls with someone for two months and they still just want to talk about their commute/ the weather. Who are these people? What is it that they do behind closed doors? They are not to be trusted.

But don't fret: we also have tips for finding housemates who suck less, which is what you're here for. Thankfully, they are short.

Don't Move in with Your Best Friends

Living with people can be difficult. If you've got a good relationship, moving in with them is only going to put pressure on it. You could be the best friends in the world, but living with people is mostly about compatibility – we'll get to that later.

Go Meet Them

Time isn't always on your side, but if you can avoid it, you should try not to move in somewhere sight-unseen. Again, it's not about conducting an investigation - more of a vibe check. Make sure they can make a good cup of tea. If they offer you homemade banana bread, you've struck gold. You don't need to know their blood type or what their parents do, just that they're not weird and, if they are, it's good weird and not disappearing-your-pets weird.

Compatibility

This is the number-one thing you're looking for. It's not about being best friends forever, it's about compatible schedules and values. If you move in with four associate lawyers, you're effectively living alone during the week. If they work in hospitality, especially nightlife, they might have an entirely different schedule to you, so you might be seeing people eating 2pm breakfasts. They're probably good fun, though. Is their home just a place to store their possessions and occasionally their sleeping body, or is it where they really live? These things are important, and it's not hard to find out enough about people to understand them.

Grind Guide #019
The Office Christmas Party

The office Christmas party – never was there a more wretched hive of scum and villainy. Most people don't have a lot of good things to say about their work Christmas party – after all, they literally have to be paid to inhabit the same space as everyone there at any other time... Still, despite the room-temperature sausage rolls, ironic Christmas sweaters, non-ironic Christmas sweaters, and colleagues with surprising opinions on what constitutes your personal space, there is normally plenty to drink – plus the chance for a fleeting dalliance with Karl from marketing. Your eyes meet across the buffet table. He smiles, and his gaze lingers, but you're not sure if it's on you or the Iceland scotch eggs. You wave, but he doesn't wave back. Time stands still. Christmas is ruined.

Lucky for you, we've thrown more than the odd party at Grind, so we daresay we know a thing or two about them. What's more, we're willing to completely make up a thing or two more. It's the time for giving, after all. So, whether you're the tragic soul lumbered with organizing your Christmas party or just looking to survive it, follow our tips to stop you from having to hide out in the stationery cupboard until it all blows over.

Actually Show Up – and Be on Time

Even if this isn't your thing – and it shouldn't be your thing – you should show up. If there's a fancy-dress theme, you should be leading the charge, not the one who's taking themselves too seriously and dialled back. Make sure you're seen there by the people who matter, and that you say thank you to whoever organized it. Don't be checking your work emails in a corner.

Down with Activities

Activities, without exception, are shit. Maybe except karaoke. What we're trying to avoid here is organized fun – that is, fun that has been organized. Fun has no schedule or itinerary, fun does what it wants. Fun fucking hates you – you're not fun's real dad, and you never will be. So, no axe-throwing, no mini-golf and absolutely no escape rooms. If we wanted to have a ridiculously dressed out-of-work actor pretend to be friends with us for 45 minutes, we'd go on a Jack the Ripper walk.

Secret Santa, Climate Criminal

Secret Santa is fun, but his days are clearly numbered. It's frankly bizarre that he's lasted this long. We're all lying to ourselves about how sustainable Christmas is: why is it we carry old shopping bags to the supermarket year-round, yet see tinsel as an inalienable human right come December? Still, tinsel can be reused and someone will inevitably create a sustainable version. Secret Santa, however, is an eco-crime.

We're not sure where it began, but today Secret Santa is effectively an opportunity to find the most useless present imaginable, laugh at it briefly, and then put it in the bin. No one ever got anything good.

Eat, Drink, Be Merry

At Christmas, as at other times, you should always be one to two drinks behind the drunkest person. That's a safe distance: you're enjoying the requisite amount of merriment, but you won't be remembered for things you don't remember. Well, except maybe for the lingering moment you shared with Karl at the buffet table earlier.

If you're organizing, Christmas is not the time to be frugal. Give the people what they want – even Scrooge bought the biggest turkey for Bob Cratchit's family.

Leave at 2am

Well, 2am at the absolute latest. Post-2am at an office party is the realm of HR inquiries, which are to be avoided – much like the people who work there.

Evenings at Grind

On weekdays, the evening is any time after work for us. It might even start at 2pm on a Friday if you're really lucky. At the weekend, we'd call it time for dinner.

At Grind, it means turning down the lights, turning up the music, and swapping our lunchier, brunchier menu for one that's a little bit more small plates and cocktails – with the occasional cheeseburger thrown in for good measure. It occupies the space in which work becomes play, and the beginning of the night ahead.

Grind Guide #020
Taking Care of Yourself Like a Grown-up

Repeat after me: 'Doing a facemask does not constitute a self-care routine.' Now we've addressed the manuka honey elephant in the room, we can move on to what does. There's a whole lot of grown-upping in this book, and no part of that is more important than taking proper care of yourself. Today, we're all wise enough to know that no man is an island and that, while support networks are important, taking time to make sure your own needs are met is an equally vital part of adult life.

Sadly, short perhaps of skincare and exercise, no subject is written about so poorly and so widely as self-care. If you ask us, self-care is about doing what makes you feel good, and acknowledging that putting yourself first isn't always selfish, but an important aspect of your existence on this little planet. The idea of anyone telling you how you should practise self-care is pretty bankrupt if you ask us, so instead we've read literally every book, article and tweet about self-care and distilled them down to help you make up your own mind. We're talking serious research; there are graphs and shit. This is the very best, and the very worst of that advice.

Light a Candle

Based on our extensive research, we've found that the likelihood of a person or company talking about candles for self-care (axis X) is directly proportional to the likelihood that they sell candles (axis Y).

While this is a red flag on the Grind Self-Care Index, we do also really like candles, as long as they're not those of a certain rancid American brand that we were absolutely sure would kill your plants until our publisher's lawyers convinced us otherwise.

Do Yoga or Other Exercise

No one can argue with this one; it's literally science. Even if you can't hack the spirituality bits of yoga, or the bro-fist bit of exercise, there's something here for you. Remember, this is for self-care, not about what you look like – so no one's telling you to do anything and it's not about some sort of bullshit routine you invent during the Sunday scaries and then beat yourself up over for the rest of the week. If you don't feel like it, don't do it.

Say No to Things

This one is an underrated gem, and isn't given nearly the credit it deserves. Just say no. It's the most liberating feeling you can have on a Friday night. It doesn't matter if you made the plans hours or months ago, just – every now and again – treat yourself to a no. Make sure to give a little notice though: not cancelling plans an hour before is the only thing separating us from the animals.

Write a Book/Learn an Instrument

This is a terrible idea. Unless you're really, really into it – and that's amazing if you are. The last thing you need for self-care is a project to beat yourself up over when you leave it unfinished. Self-care is a marathon, not a sprint, but it's one of small random steps. On a Sunday night, when everything is possible, we all love to indulge fantasies of being fluent in Portuguese or a master on the piano, but by Monday morning you'll only be haunted by the Duolingo owl as another app gathers dust on your phone. By all means, write, draw, sing, but don't write cheques your body can't cash, Maverick. For younger readers, that was a reference to the popular 1986 action movie *Top Gun*.

Grind Guide #021
How to Host a Dinner Party

Frankie from Grind HQ says 'a night in is the new night out', like some sort of strange recluse. It's not just her, though. Having quizzed everyone from the recluses to those who haven't seen a home-cooked meal outside of *Come Dine with Me* for about a decade, we've got a list of tips for putting on the perfect dinner party.

Preparation

My English teacher once told me that 'failing to prepare is preparing to fail', but then she also thought that Piggy from *Lord of the Flies* was some sort of Jesus symbol and liked the work of Carol Ann Duffy, so what does she know? Sadly, though, this is pretty good advice when it comes to making food. Frankie says that deciding on a theme or type of cuisine – even if super vague – is the best way to get started. We guess that means fairy lights and sombreros.

Prioritization

Before you start noting down ingredients for Ottolenghi's pappardelle with rose harissa, take a breath and think about logistics. Unless you went to cookery school, you're not going to be able to go all out on every course, so pace yourself. If you're going to spend three hours on a twice-baked-white-chocolate-cheesecake – which sounds fucking disgusting, by the way – just choose something simple for the main, so you're not tied to the oven all night.

Level Four Vegan

At Grind, we literally ask every single guest about their allergies just to be safe. While you might know them already, these days checking in with people's dietary requirements is a pretty good habit to get into if you're cooking for others, especially if it's a large group or people you don't know so well. Cooking is one of those strange pastimes that somehow is all about you, but also all about them. If you move in the unfortunate circles that we do, there'll inevitably be two vegans, a coeliac, a coelacanth, and someone who's only eating coal this week. If someone has decided to show up while on a juice cleanse, you are welcome to strike them from the Christmas list. Insufferable.

Timing

Frankie says you should work out how long you expect all your preparations to take, and then times that by two, as you'll inevitably miss off an ingredient or forget to turn the oven on. Yeah, we know: we thought she was supposed to be good at this, too. Anyway, if you do that, the worst that can happen is that you'll be ready early and can spend a little more time talking to your guests and having a glass of wine. Look at you, you're a veritable Nigella.

Style over Substance, Always

In advice that has no whisper of endorsement from any of the people who cook professionally at Grind or elsewhere:
if it looks good, people will probably forget it tastes bad. Obviously, we want you to try your best – in an ideal world we'd all be making fresh pasta and serving homemade gelato. But life gets in the way, and you sometimes have other fish to fry, even if they're only metaphorical. If it comes down to it, just make sure it looks amazing.

Ambience

We know better than anyone that if there's two things that will make or break a dinner party, it's the lighting and the music. The music is easy: create a dinner-party playlist, and then leave it alone. There is nothing worse than a night spent listening to the first 45 seconds of 'Africa' by Toto, interrupted by someone requesting 'Want You Back' by Haim through the medium of bellowing at Alexa.

In terms of lighting, unless you're made of money, stock up on tealights, baby. None of the ones with the metal cups, mind you – this is a sustainable affair, and you can get wax-only ones now. You'll spend a little time cleaning it off the crockery, but the turtles will thank you.

Snatching Victory from the Jaws of Defeat

Sometimes, things don't go to plan. When that happens, it's important to remember that your guests probably still love you and don't mind nearly as much as you do. Dry your tears, order a pizza, open another bottle of wine, and try again another time.

Grind Fish Fingers

Yeah, just two ingredients. That's like three ingredients less than Jamie Oliver.

Anyway, this is another of our favourites. It's a great little small plate, perfect with cocktails or beers or just about anything. There are loads of wonderful food ideas that get a bad rap because we're used to seeing them in the freezer aisle. There's no reason fish fingers (fish sticks) can't be something special – and pretty healthy too – if you just invest a little time and attention.

Serves 2

500g (1lb 2oz) potatoes – we use Agria potatoes, but you can use any medium to large floury potato. If it makes a good roast potato, it works for us.
250g (9oz) smoked haddock
vegetable oil, for frying
sea salt and black pepper

Serving options: mayonnaise, hot sauce, chives

Heat your oven to 160°C (320°F).

Put your potatoes whole and unpeeled in a large pan of water, enough to cover them completely and boil with the lid on. There, that was a strong start.

You're looking to get them al dente, which will take about 5 minutes if you're using the kind of potatoes you might make a baked potato from – but more or less time depending on size.

Meanwhile, season the smoked haddock and cook it in the middle of the oven for 4 minutes. The smoked haddock you get from the fishmonger or the supermarket is basically cooked already, so we're really just warming this up and making it easier to break apart.

Prick the potatoes with a sharp knife to check for done-ness. The skin should tear easily and the inside should be getting soft – not soft like mashed potato, but a little softer than they started. Once done, remove the potatoes from the hot water – carefully, mind you, and leave them to cool.

Your smoked haddock will be done by now, so remove from the oven and flake it into a large bowl,

discarding the skin. Remember, we're looking to break rather than mash it up, so be gentle. Leave the oven on – we're going to need it in a moment.

Peel your potatoes now that – like me – they're not so hot-to-handle as they once were. Then grate them into the bowl with the fish.

Season and mix your bowl of fish and potato, spread it all in an even 2.5cm (1in) thick layer on to a baking tray lined with baking paper, then bake at the top of the oven for 15 minutes.

Now, we give you options! At this point, you can either remove it from the oven, let it cool and even chill for a rainy day, or you can crack on.

When you're ready to cook, slice the baked mix into chunky fingers and fry them in a pan with a splash of oil. Keep turning the fingers until they're crispy and golden brown.

We serve these with mustard mayonnaise, but regular mayo is just as good. Alternatively, try the Grind Korean Hot Sauce that we put on our Fried Chicken Sandwich (p74).

Padrón Peppers

Padróns, small Spanish peppers fried in oil until blistered, are almost too easy to warrant a recipe, but they're definitely a dinner-party essential. In the last few years they've gone from tapas bars to just about everywhere, probably in no small part due to our friends at Soho House, who serve them all over the place. Best of all, it means they're also more available in supermarkets, which they never used to be.

You can make yours even better with a garnish, even if it's just lime wedges, crispy shallots and toasted sesame seeds like we use. Pictured on p103.

Serves 2

vegetable oil, for frying
120g (4¼oz) padrón peppers
sea salt
1 lime, half juiced, half cut
    into wedges

Garnishes: lime wedges, crispy
    shallots, toasted sesame seeds

In a pan on a high heat, heat a splash of oil until it just begins to smoke.

Sauté your peppers in the hot oil, keeping it on a high heat – you'll want to keep them moving and turning.

Once your peppers are browned and almost beginning to blacken, sprinkle some sea salt on to them and remove from the heat.

Put the peppers in a bowl or on a small plate, dress with the juice of half a lime, and garnish with a lime wedge and whatever else you like.

Courgette Fritti,
lemon, tofu aioli

These come on and off the menu at Grind with the seasons – summer is really the moment for courgettes (zucchini) – but we really wish they were there year-round. There's just something so moreish about them, like fries or onion rings, but with the added bonus that they're not going to kill you. Today, the Grind menu is more plant-based than ever, but it wasn't until we added these that we really got plant-based snacks for cocktails right. If you can get the batter nice and crisp, they're perfect. Pictured on p103.

Serves 2

For the courgette and lemon
45g (1½oz) gluten-free flour
60ml (2fl oz) white wine
1 courgette (zucchini) – a large one
1 lemon
vegetable oil, for deep frying
1 pinch sumac, to garnish

For the aioli
300g (10½oz) silken tofu
1 clove garlic, crushed
1 lemon, juiced
½ tsp turmeric powder
150ml (5fl oz) vegetable oil
1 pinch salt

Whisk the flour and wine to make a light batter. There's always something kind of weird about mixing flour and wine in my head, but maybe that's just me.

Slice your courgette (zucchini) and lemon into skinny slices, 5mm (¼in) thick. You can go a little chunkier if you like, like an onion ring, but they hold a lot more moisture than an onion so there's a risk they'll go a little soggy.

Batter your slices with your flour and wine mix.

If you're using a deep fryer, fry these at 160°C (320°F) for 2 minutes, and then at 180°C (365°F) for just a few seconds to crisp them up. If you don't have a deep fryer, half-fill a large, heavy-based pan with vegetable oil and put over a high heat until a breadcrumb dropped in the oil quickly sizzles and rises to the surface. Add the battered slices to the fryer or pan in batches and cook until golden brown.

Remove your slices using a slotted spoon, drain on a plate lined with paper towels and keep them warm. In the meantime, throw your tofu, garlic, lemon juice, turmeric, oil and salt into a blender and blitz until smooth.

Easy peasy. Garnish as you like: we use a bit of sumac for colour and flavour.

Grind Guide #022
Politely Bailing on Your Date

So, you matched with someone last week and things have been going well. That, or they might just have a really nice dog – it's just so hard to tell sometimes. You've been talking and you've put something in your diary. You might have even picked out a place that you think is dimly lit enough for you to pretend to be who you are on Instagram. But now the date has crept up, you want to take a rain check. We've all been there.

Maybe you have better plans, maybe you're not feeling it, maybe you've realized the dog wasn't even theirs, but tonight just isn't for you. The thing is, you can count the hours between now and your impending date on one hand. What you do here is up to you, but ghosting them really isn't cool. Here are some pointers from our team, who have experienced a few stood-up dates in their time, first- and second-hand.

Too Hot / Too Cold / Environmental Factors
The lowest of the low. This is the toilet of excuses, and you should hang your head in shame. According to science that we made up and didn't care to validate, London is arguably the most temperately miserable city on Earth, so unless he or she is from the other side of the world, this isn't going to fly – and rightly so.

You Need to Be There for a Friend

This one is an old favourite, and reflects pretty well on you as an individual. While you're arguably taking a moral high ground, it's mostly in the delivery, and they're probably going to see through it – so don't expect a text back.

The Double Booking

One of our baristas had a tried-and-tested method of ridding himself of an unwanted companion come morning by telling them he had to go out for breakfast for his mum's birthday – guaranteed to empty his flat in record time. It went really well until he used it twice with the same guy.

You're Sick, and You Don't Want to Make Them Sick Too

This one always scores low for imagination, but is at least difficult to argue with. For extra points, this doubles up as a great test further down the line: if they offer to bring you soup, you know it's love.

Just Go Anyway

The wildcard answer, and the one you should be doing. Go and live a little!

Grind Guide #023
Buying and Drinking Wine Like a Grown-up

There used to be an off-licence over the road from Shoreditch Grind that sold two bottles of wine for a fiver. You weren't even allowed to buy just one: it had to be two – which admittedly worked out nicely as there were two flavours, red and white. Was this good wine? Possibly not. But it was a good deal, and the place did dry cleaning, too.

Now, we know we said that coffee was the quintessential grown-up beverage, but that was 76 pages ago – we were young then, and full of hope. Legally speaking, wine is quite literally an adult beverage, but there's also something grown-up about knowing just a little bit about it. Much like coffee, wine is loaded with bullshit, most of which started as interesting knowledge and tidbits, but sadly turned into excuses for gatekeeping and point-scoring. So, we'll leave identifying Left Bank Bordeaux from Right Bank for another book, and start at the beginning.

Wine is grown and enjoyed all over the world and, contrary to the belief of this book's sponsor, fits into literally every social occasion. Like coffee, wine is best enjoyed socially – whether that's buck's fizz on Christmas morning, goon sacks in a grotty Australian hostel, or just good, old-fashioned orange-rind-and-stale-bread prison hooch.

But for those in the back, let's start with the basics. You have grapes, which are grown, picked, juiced, fermented, bottled and then enjoyed with much merriment. There are only red wine grapes and white wine grapes. Using those two, we can make red wine, white wine, rosé wine, and, rather trendily, orange wine. White wine usually has all the skins and seeds removed, red wine has them left on – and rosé has something in between, depending on who makes it.

If the wine you're drinking while reading this is sparkling, which is French for 'fizzy', it's either naturally carbonated in the bottle over a period of time, or been fizzed up in a tank – a more recent innovation. Generally, more expensive wines are carbonated in the bottle with a secondary fermentation, while cheaper sparkling wine is mass-produced in tanks – quite fitting considering that it's also mass-consumed over brunch. As ever, there are exceptions, but that's the gist of it.

Wine is grown and produced in lots of countries, but you'll often see people talking about the 'old world' and 'new world' and – like me – you'll be disappointed to discover it has nothing to do with the direct-to-video sequel to *Pocahontas*. Not unlike the movie, though, this naming convention seems in pretty poor taste to us, but just so you know, what's called the 'old world' typically covers wines from Europe and 'new world' is everywhere else. Yeah, we have no idea how this is still a thing, either.

In terms of actual, meaningful differences, if you're going to make sweeping generalizations, you could say that winemaking in Europe is more rooted in tradition. Over hundreds of years, some of these traditions have been enshrined in the laws regulating what wines can and cannot be called, based on how and where they're grown.

What all this means for you, or for anyone, is that you can learn something about wine by reading a book. There are facts you'll know already, such as Champagne has to be from the Champagne region, and facts you might not – like how Sauvignon Blanc from New Zealand is, broadly speaking, Um Bongo. But, just like with coffee, the best way to learn is just to try lots and lots of it, and figure out your own rules for yourself.

Here are some of ours to get you started. Some can be bent, others can be broken.

- If you are going to buy more than one glass of the same wine, buy a bottle. Always. It is known.

- The thing people say about the second wine from the bottom of the list being the cheapest because restaurants know people won't order the bottom one is a myth. We should know, we literally write them.

- Wine that is acidic generally tastes good with food that is high in fat or protein. This one's less opinion, and more about food science – but try it out.

- The whole red wine with meat, white wine with fish thing is more memorable than useful.

- Ordering a 'dry white wine' is good in a pinch, but also covers a vast swathe of wine styles, so it's basically wheel of fortune.

- Most importantly, ask questions. In our long and storied experience, people who work with wine drink quite a lot of it, and will be excited to help you find something you like, and then drink it for you if you don't.

Grind Guide #024
After-Work Drinks

Movies would really like you to think that the decisions that matter are made in shiny glass boardrooms with too much air-conditioning, but this is London, and more often than not, they're made in the pub.

The ancient Chinese military strategist Sun Tzu once said, 'the art of war is to subdue the enemy without fighting', which is probably a useful tip if you're trying to unite China in 250 BC, but kind of irrelevant to doing shots of tequila at 2am on a Tuesday night in Soho. Still, you'll make the best friends you'll ever have doing just that, so here are some tips.

Act Like You've Been There Before

It doesn't matter if you're sitting on the front row at fashion week or in a snooker hall in some miserable shithole, it's a lot better for everyone involved if you play it cool and behave like you've done this a million times before. Everybody hates a tourist. Whatever you do, don't take photos of cocktails, or anything else for that matter.

Growing Up

As the years pass, you begin to realize that no one settles down as they get older, they just get better at hiding a hangover, especially if you're with people who work in restaurants and hospitality – those guys are bulletproof. Still, the first and last rule of after-work drinks is make sure you're the first one in the following morning, even if you're still drunk.

Don't Offer or Try to Buy Drinks for Your Manager

They know you can't afford it, you're not impressing anyone – as ever, it's best to not look too rich to the people who decide how much money you make. If your CEO wanted a tequila shot, they'd order one.

Get in, Loser

If you're at a party big enough – or work somewhere small enough – that your CEO or creative director is there, then your boss's boss's boss is always the gauge for any kind of debauchery. If they're not drinking, you're not drinking – but if it's beginning to look like the last days of Rome, then get in, loser. A fashion designer who'll remain nameless once got carried out of Shoreditch Grind at 3am, riding on a tide of his crying interns. It was **glorious.**

Grind Guide #025

Surviving the Holidays, or Why *Love Actually* is the Best and Worst Movie Ever Made

Contrary to the belief of all internet journalists with a deadline and word count to hit, being single at Christmas really isn't as literally the worst as people tell you. *Love Actually* made a good point that Christmas is a great time to have someone to love in your life, but it also thought recording your best friend's wedding while following his wife around like you're making a K-pop fancam was an appropriate – and daresay romantic – thing to do. Family-wise, you'll maybe get a question or two from the more distant rellies, but they're just trying to engage with you and it's the way they know how. 'Is there someone special in your life?' is a game that has been played between uncles, aunties, nieces and nephews since the dawn of time, and one day you'll be on the other end of it. It's all quite wholesome, really.

Seriously though, let's get down to the real nitty-gritty about Christmas. And by Christmas, we mean rating the plot lines of *Love Actually* on a scale of one Karl to five Karls.

- Nearly two decades on, we're honestly not sure the whole Colin Firth section wasn't just elaborate fan fiction to get him into a lake like in the '90s *Pride and Prejudice* TV series. That said, Colin has an excellent navy blue cable-knit sweater. **3/5 Karls**

- Does Chiwetel Ejiofor ever find out about Keira Knightley kissing his best friend? Why does she kiss him in the first place? Also, the panelled, knitted, zip-up sweater that Andrew Lincoln wears when she discovers his creepy video is unforgivable. **1/5 Karls**

- What are Martin Freeman and Joanna Page actually doing in their naked scenes together? Were they making porn and we just didn't realize this whole time? The assumption was they were body doubles for another movie – but that sex scene seems to really go on, and we've watched *Game of Thrones*. **2/5 Karls**

- Karl from the office is a good-looking guy. Sadly, when Laura Linney's character is called at just the wrong moment by her brother at the hospital, Karl's reaction is not good. That's not going to cut it any more, Karl. **0/5 Karls**

- No score at all for Colin from the BT adverts going to America and sleeping with January Jones. In this house, we refuse to acknowledge this ever happened. Disqualified from receiving any Karls.

- Emma Thompson and Alan Rickman's scenes are about as heartbreaking as you can get, but we should have seen it coming in his overall creepiness from the beginning. That said, someone really needs to call HR about Mia. **4/5 Karls**

- The whole thing with Liam Neeson and his son is heartwarming, but suddenly we're confronted with the object of the son's affections singing the worst cover ever of 'All I Want for Christmas Is You'. Bonus points for Liam Neeson being a great dad. **3/5 Karls**

- Hugh Grant knocking on doors on Christmas Eve is the highlight of my festive season every year, as is the scene in the car with the child dressed as an octopus. Not the Prime Minister we deserve, but the Prime Minister we need. **5/5 Karls**

- Ageing rock star Bill Nighy declaring his platonic love for his manager, having spent the whole movie promoting his terrible Christmas song, is the heart and soul of Christmas. Honourable mention for portrayals of male friendship also go to Bill Nighy in *About Time* ten years later. Bill, you'll always have **5/5 Karls** from me; Christmas truly is all around us.

Christmas small-talk is the worst small-talk – here's a primer for getting through it.

- You've had 'a great year, thanks'.

- *Love Actually* is the best Christmas movie, see above.

- *Die Hard* is not a Christmas movie, it's an action movie set at Christmas. There are many sequels and they are about action, and not about Christmas. We watched them to verify this fact.

Grind Guide #026
Making Cocktails at Home

There's a theory that the reason our late-stage monkey ancestors came down from the trees was to eat fermented fallen fruit on the ground, because it gave them a buzz. We've crawled out of a few primordial oozes ourselves in order to go to brunch, so that sounds pretty plausible to us.

What we know for sure is that humans have been drinking for a long time, so in much the same way that you have a toaster for making toast, having the bare necessities for making cocktails at home can be quite useful. There's a joke in there somewhere about honouring your ancestors, but this is basically just about having a good time.

Most of us have a collection of un-drunk spirits at home, but it only takes a few things to ascend from shelf of shame to gentleman's drinking cabinet, and just a few more to create a home bar of your own. Let's go through the basics.

The Tools of the Trade

These are a mix of absolute must-haves, a few things you can probably hack together in your kitchen, and things you have already but are called different things in a bar – because, y'know, bartenders. You can also pick up a kit of them all for next to nothing.

- **Jigger**. This is bartender for 'measure' and while it's a pretty essential tool, you can use anything as long as it can measure down to about 15ml (½fl oz). Just like baking or making coffee, preparing a great cocktail is all about following a recipe. Most proper jiggers measure 25ml (1fl oz) and 50ml (2fl oz) – that's a single and double shot – and some will have lines to show 15ml (½fl oz) and 35ml (1¼fl oz) as well.

- **Shaker**. This is the obvious one, but you can use almost anything as long as it's sealable. There are several different styles, but the important thing is that it lets you shake ice and liquid without having to repaint your kitchen.

- **Strainer**. A hawthorn is the type of metal strainer with the springs round the edge – you've probably seen one before and they generally come with a cocktail shaker. As you'd imagine, it keeps all the ice and other gubbins back in the shaker and out of your drink. This is pretty vital.

- **Fine strainer**. This is like a cute baby sieve (sooo kawaii). It looks a bit like an old tea strainer and, like one of those, keeps things out of your drink – except it is much more effective with little bits, such as the shards of ice created when you shake a drink. Some drinks, such as the Espresso Martini, need double straining, while others, like the Margarita, don't.

- **Bar spoon**. This is a long spoon with a mysteriously twisted handle. It's helpful for measuring out small amounts of liquids, stirring drinks and, very occasionally, when you need to float one liquid on top of another.

Beyond these, there are only a handful of other items used in this book and others. There's the 'mixing tin', but that is pretty self explanatory. If you find a recipe that asks for one, you can definitely just use a bowl, jug or big glass. There's also the muddler, which sounds like a forgetful Batman villain, but is in fact a plastic or metal tool used for crushing fruit, herbs or anything else in your drink. You can substitute just about anything for this – a spoon, or the handle of something else, even just your hands.

Of course, the most important thing is to practise – and persevere a little. Like most things, cocktails are easier than they look. You'll be shaking like the best of them in no time.

The Grind Espresso Martini

It's not a big mystery how we make the Grind Espresso Martini. There's no secret recipe and no secret sauce to it – unless you count our espresso (which you probably should). If you didn't know already, the Grind Espresso Martini is our signature – our baby, you could say. By that we mean we make a lot of them – like, a lot.

The story of the Grind Espresso Martini goes way, way back to Shoreditch Grind in 2011, when we first decided to turn what was then a little espresso bar into a cocktail joint. And, just like at 5am at any house party, we kind of ended up making do with what we had on hand. Fortunately, that was our Grind House Blend Espresso (p45), which was a pretty good place to start.

We'd had Espresso Martinis before – they're a classic – but back then we didn't realize how many corners were being cut in making them, even in the best places. You see, keeping a proper coffee machine clean and running is a lot of work, and even with the best intentions, standards can slip. After Espresso Martinis were invented in the '90s, bars first tried using bottled espresso – a pretty miserable fate for coffee. Before long, all sorts of grisly concoctions of E-number flavourings and preservatives were being used. So by the time 2011 came around, even the places we had trusted for a good drink were serving something a far throw from what we imagine genius bartender Dick Bradsell had invented all those years ago. But we didn't know any of that yet.

What we did know was that we had a killer espresso. Even then, it still took us a long time to get the balance of espresso, vodka and sugar just right. The rest is history – even if we can't remember pretty chunky sections of it. Probably for the best.

Makes 1
25ml (1fl oz) Grind House Blend
    Espresso
40ml (1½fl oz) vodka
20ml (¾fl oz) sugar syrup – that's
    just sugar dissolved in hot water
    at a one-to-one ratio (see p147)
ice

Glass: champagne coupe
Garnish: coffee beans

Pour the espresso, vodka and sugar syrup into a shaker.

Fill with ice and shake vigorously. It'll take ten seconds with a good shake – you'll know when it's ready, because there'll be a creamy head on it when you peek inside the shaker.

Double-strain into a chilled champagne coupe.

Garnish with the coffee beans, then serve and make another one.

Once, at Grind's fifth birthday party, we decided to give away 500 of these in an hour. By the time we were done, we'd had too many, and announced we were giving away another 500 more. It's safe to say no sleep was had.

Hot Flat White Russian

The Hot Flat White Russian is a Grind original – invented by Rik, our very first bartender at Shoreditch Grind back in 2012. It's not changed much over the years, besides the move from dairy to oat milk. As you might imagine, it's a twist on the White Russian made famous by Jeff Bridges' the Dude in *The Big Lebowski*, which is in turn a twist on the Black Russian, a particularly punchy classic cocktail of vodka and coffee liqueur.

This one's more of a nightcap than the Espresso Martini – even without dairy it's still got a big hot-cup-of-cocoa vibe about it. Despite all that espresso, it's a real sleepy one.

Makes 1

20ml (¾fl oz) vodka

20ml (¾fl oz) Tia Maria – or other coffee liqueur

25ml (1fl oz) Grind House Blend Espresso

150ml (6fl oz) oat milk

Glass: large latte glass or mug

Pour the vodka, coffee liqueur, your shot of espresso, and a dash of cold milk into your glass or mug and give it a quick stir.

Steam your milk, just like you would when making a coffee. You're looking for that flat white 'microfoam' that's thicker and lighter than milk, but not the froth you find on a cappuccino.

Pour into the glass, as you would for a flat white or latte.

Espresso Old Fashioned and Hot Flat White Russian

Espresso Old Fashioned

This is the third of our coffee cocktails, and the second Grind original – it was invented by Sam, who made drinks hot and cold at just about every Grind for the best part of a decade. It was originally named the 'Old Street Fashioned', after our east London home, but we figured it was better to give it a more descriptive title.

This one is a twist on possibly the most classic of classic cocktails (see p131), with the espresso a bold addition. The chocolate bitters give it an almost Christmassy feel. Surprisingly warming for a drink with ice in it. Pictured on p126.

Makes 1

50ml (2fl oz) bourbon

15ml (½fl oz) Grind House Blend Espresso

15ml (½fl oz) brown sugar syrup (see p147)

2 dashes chocolate bitters

ice

Glass: rocks glass
Garnish: orange twist

Throw it all in. Seriously, the bourbon, then the espresso, sugar syrup and the bitters – you can't go wrong. Well, maybe with that last bit – just two little dashes.

Stir with ice until chilled. You don't need a lot of ice here, just enough to reach the top of the liquid. Also, you don't have to rush this bit – you're looking for some of the ice to melt and dilute things a little.

Strain into a rocks glass over fresh ice and garnish with an orange twist.

Remember, you've got some dilution from the stirring, so don't worry if you get more liquid out than you put in.

Tommy's Margarita

Definitely a Grind favourite, this is particularly moreish. The Tommy's Margarita was invented in San Francisco when Julio Bermejo, working at his parents' Mexican restaurant, swapped the orange liqueur used in the original version for agave syrup. Unlike most twists on classics, this one isn't that much of a departure, but it's a definite improvement. The Tommy's is the only Margarita you'll ever need – besides, perhaps, the Picante popularized by our friends at Soho House. That's just the same as a Tommy's, with half a chilli added. Pictured on p133.

Makes 1
50ml (2fl oz) tequila
25ml (1fl oz) lime juice
15ml (½oz) agave syrup
ice

Glass: rocks glass
Garnish: lime slice

Pour all three liquid ingredients into a shaker and fill it with good-quality ice.

Yeah, we didn't always know ice could be good and bad. Good ice is all about the speed at which it melts in a drink – you're looking for cubes with a low surface area, and no bubbles, so you should be able to see through it like glass. You can make great ice in your freezer at home, and the ingredients are free, but if you're short on time, we'll forgive you for buying it from the supermarket.

Shake it all up. You're looking for 15 seconds of good, vigorous shaking, so break a sweat.

Strain into a rocks glass with fresh ice. You don't need to worry about double straining this, so you can probably do it one-handed if you're showing off.

Negroni

The Espresso Martini, the Negroni and the Tommy's were where it all started for Grind cocktails, and all three have been on the menu ever since. The Negroni is a perfect all-night drink, not heady enough to put you on the floor, and not too sweet, either. Like so many other classic cocktails, the origin of this one is more of a myth than anything else. Legend has it that in 1919, Italy's Count Negroni asked a bartender to strengthen an Americano – another classic cocktail – by using gin instead of soda water (club soda).

The Negroni is Grind founder David's favourite cocktail, quite possibly because his dad and dad's friends would pretty much force-feed them to him from a young, but entirely legal, age. It's something of an acquired taste, but once you get into them, nothing else quite works the same. It's also three ingredients, so it's basically un-fuck-up-able, even in the diviest of dive bars. Pictured on p132.

Makes 1
25ml (1fl oz) gin
25ml (1fl oz) Campari
25ml (1fl oz) sweet vermouth
ice

Glass: rocks glass
Garnish: orange slice

Pour the gin, Campari and vermouth into a mixing glass – or just the bottom half of a shaker if that's all you've got handy – fill with ice and stir.

You're looking to mix the drink, chill it and add a little water for dilution as the ice melts – so give it a good 15 seconds of stirring.

Strain into a rocks glass over fresh ice. We garnish ours with a slice of orange, for nutritional value, or something like that.

Old Fashioned

About as classic as they come. If James Bond really existed, this is what he would drink – because a vodka martini, when shaken and not stirred, is a revolting watery concoction and you shouldn't trust anyone who tells you otherwise. Pictured on p132.

Makes 1
50ml (2fl oz) bourbon
2 tsp brown sugar syrup (see p147)
1 dash bitters
ice

Glass: rocks glass
Garnish: orange twist

Pour the bourbon, sugar syrup and your dash of bitters into a mixing glass – or just the bottom half of a shaker if that's all you've got handy – and stir.

You're looking to mix the drink, chill it and add a little water for dilution as the ice melts – so give it a good 15 seconds of stirring.

Strain into a rocks glass over fresh ice.

Aperol Spritz

A drink that needs no introduction. Drink it over breakfast, drink it in the bath. Pictured on p133.

Makes 1

50ml (2fl oz) Aperol

75ml (3fl oz) prosecco

75ml (3fl oz) soda water (club soda)
 – which is just fizzy water that
 takes itself too seriously

ice

Glass: whatever you like – put it in
 a wine glass, put it in a bucket,
 inject it into your veins

Garnish: orange slice, if you like

Pour the Aperol, prosecco and soda water (club soda) into your chalice of choice.

Add ice, and lots of it, right up to the top. Give it a quick stir. Unlike the Negroni or Old Fashioned, you're not going for dilution this time, but just chilling it.

Throw in a straw, maybe an orange slice for a balanced diet and all that.

Pornstar Martini

We didn't want to put this concoction in the book, but sometimes you just have to give the people what they want. There will be nights in your life when you will be Hendrix, when you will be Nick Cave, when you will be Frankie Knuckles. But tonight you are a wedding DJ, and you are playing the 'Macarena'. Pictured on p132.

Makes 1
35ml (1¼fl oz) vanilla vodka
15ml (½fl oz) passion fruit liqueur
50ml (2fl oz) passion fruit purée
15ml (½fl oz) pineapple juice
ice
25ml (1fl oz) prosecco

Glass: champagne coupe or glass, plus a shot glass for the prosecco
Garnish: passion fruit half

Pour the vodka, passion fruit liqueur and purée, pineapple juice and your last sliver of self-respect into a shaker, fill it with ice, and shake the pain away.

Double strain into your glass – that means use the regular strainer as well as the cute little baby sieve (see p123).

Garnish with half a passion fruit and serve it with the shot of prosecco on the side. Don't you dare pull any bullshit like setting it on fire or putting a fucking sparkler in it.

Grind by Night

In 1957, Nappy Brown sang 'Night Time Is the Right Time', and you know what? We think Nappy might have been on to something.

For us, night-time starts after dinner – or if it's a particularly good night, dinner turns into night-time and catches you unawares. At Grind, we'd probably have to define it as the point where cocktails over dinner turn into cocktails over cocktails, which you'll find is a pretty natural progression. For us that means the lights go a little lower and the music gets a little louder, but for you it could mean just about anything. The world is your oyster.

Grind Guide #027
Making Room for Dessert

Where there's a will, there's a way. A bit of gelato to finish you off? You're probably all right. Sticky coffee pudding with cream and ice cream? More of a challenge. Nonetheless, the struggle of how to make room for pudding is something we think people might need a little bit of guidance on.

Guilt-Free Since '93

Yeah, we really have to leave this one behind. If you ask us, dessert doesn't mean gorging yourself at the trough of your wanton desires, but rather basking in the warm glow of practising self-care. Ease your woes; there should be no embarrassment about the fact that you abso-fucking-lutely would like to see the pudding menu. Worry not, put the looming societal guilt out of the equation, and we're sure you'll find there's a little more room than you first expected.

Make Room

This one requires a little preparation, but dessert is not the time to be wearing something tight-fitting. If the body can make room to accommodate eight to 12 mochis, your wardrobe should too. If you're out, desperate and need an immediate fix, then Emma from Grind HQ says you can always just undo your top button – although please never mention this was her advice as it's not very cool.

Some Actual, Practical, Grown-up Advice

Share your pudding. While your immediate, greedy self might want whatever the menu offers in the heat of the moment, the best desserts are sometimes just a cup of coffee and a taste of something sweet. Better yet, if you're on a date, order for the two of you and let the other person eat it.

No Regrets

Whatever you do, don't regret it. You're going to die one day and food is a delight – and delights are not to be compromised on. Say yes, own it, and get on with your life.

Grind House
Blend Tiramisu

It's safe to say most people choose cocktails over dessert at Grind, but this one's a splash of vodka away from being an edible Espresso Martini.

Serving a couple of million cups of espresso a year, we've really no excuses when it comes to making a killer tiramisu. Despite the dessert's Italian origins, you'll find that a terrifying number of recipes use filter coffee rather than espresso.

Surprisingly, tiramisu is quite a recent invention – only dating back to the '60s.

The name literally means 'pick me up' in Italian, but much like that phrase in English, it can refer to either waking you up or just lifting your mood. With 12 shots of espresso in this one, we'd bet on it.

Serves 4

For the custard
5 egg yolks
130g (4¾oz) caster (superfine) sugar
300ml (10½fl oz) double (heavy) cream
330g (11½oz) mascarpone

For the coffee syrup
300ml (10½fl oz) Grind House Blend Espresso – that's about 12 shots
200ml (7fl oz) Tia Maria – or other coffee liqueur
75ml (3fl oz) sugar syrup (see p147)

To assemble
200g (7oz) ladyfingers
cocoa powder, for dusting

First, we'll make the custard. In a heatproof bowl set over a pan of gently simmering water, mix the egg yolks and sugar and whisk them until you get the consistency of whipped cream – so, closer to thick mayonnaise than to ketchup.

Add the double (heavy) cream and mascarpone and mix until you have a smooth custard. If it makes peaks, you've probably gone too far!

Cool, and then chill – the custard, we mean. But you do that too.

Assuming you've just made the custard, as well as the coffee and sugar syrup, you're going to want them all to cool to at least room temperature. Make yourself a drink while you wait.

For the coffee syrup, stir the espresso, Tia Maria and sugar syrup in a large bowl.

Add your ladyfingers to the bowl. You want them to absorb the liquid, but not to go mushy – give them 20 seconds to begin with and keep an eye on them.

Arrange some of the soaked fingers in a layer on the bottom of whatever you're planning on serving this in. We make them in coffee cups, but you can just as easily make a big one in a baking tin or a trifle bowl as shown here.

Add a layer of custard, then repeat until you've used up all your fingers and custard. Chill these in the fridge until you're ready to serve them, and then dust with cocoa powder before serving. Remember, the longer you leave them in the fridge, the mushier they'll get – but that's a preference thing more than anything.

Vegan Chocolate Mousse,
honeycomb & raspberries

Our chocolate mousse, albeit in its vegan form, is a relatively new addition to the menu at Grind but has become a bit of a firm favourite. Without the milk to play with, this one can get seriously rich, so fortunately these will last you all week in the fridge.

You can try making the honeycomb yourself, but it's a bit fiddly and you can pick it up in the supermarket. We'd really recommend frozen raspberries too, for a little sweetness.

Serves 4

150g (5½oz) good-quality dark chocolate
½ tsp vanilla essence
110ml (3¾fl oz) aquafaba – chickpea (garbanzo bean) liquid from the can
70g (2½oz) caster (superfine) sugar
80ml (3fl oz) coconut cream

Garnish: frozen raspberries, mint, honeycomb

Place a heatproof bowl over a pan of water and bring the water to a gentle simmer. Break the chocolate into pieces in the bowl, add the vanilla essence and allow to melt. Alternatively, just do it the lazy way in a bowl in the microwave.

Whisk the aquafaba in a large mixing bowl until it becomes stiff peaks. This is a lot of whisking, so use a stand mixer if you have one or an electric hand whisk if not. Add the sugar and continue to whisk until it looks like meringue.

Once the chocolate is melted, add the coconut cream, mix, and then gently fold in your aquafaba meringue until evenly distributed.

Portion the mix into bowls or glasses, leave them to cool to room temperature, then put them in the fridge. They'll take an hour or two to set.

Eat whenever you fancy. They're great in the middle of the night with frozen raspberries and mint. We garnish them with a little broken honeycomb, which is great too!

Sticky Coffee Pudding

As any great chef will tell you, the very best recipes start with a strong pun and work backwards from there – we used to have a fig cocktail called Notorious F.I.G. for the same reason, but it just wasn't very nice.

When you get your ingredients together – your *mise en place* if you're feeling continental and sophisticated – you'll probably think that this looks like a terrifying amount of dates, but worry not. Speaking of dates, try to get the Medjool ones if you're really pushing things out there, or if you're just made of money. They're bigger and softer than regular dates and have a rich, caramelly flavour.

Serves 4

275g (9¾oz) dates – about 250g (9oz) once pitted
400ml (14fl oz) water
½ tsp bicarbonate of soda (baking soda)
100g (3½oz) butter, softened – plus extra for greasing
90g (3¼oz) caster (superfine) sugar
1 tsp salt
4 tsp baking powder
2 medium or large eggs
125g (4½oz) plain (all-purpose) flour
15g (½oz) cornflour (cornstarch)
clotted cream, to serve (optional)

For the Grind Coffee Sauce
225g (8oz) dark brown sugar
50g (1¾oz) butter
100ml (3½fl oz) double (heavy) cream
50ml (2fl oz) Grind House Blend Espresso or black coffee

Add the pitted dates and water to a saucepan and bring to the boil.

Add the bicarbonate of soda (baking soda) and wait for it to be incorporated. The mix will turn slightly green – strange, we know – and then turn dark. Remove from the heat and allow to cool, even just for a few minutes.

Put the whole lot in a blender and blitz until thicker than ketchup, but still very much a liquid.

Put the butter, sugar, salt and half the baking powder in a large mixing bowl and mix until it's a thick and consistent texture.

Gradually add the eggs one at a time while mixing. Don't worry if the mixture gets a little lumpy here, but try to keep it from getting stuck to the sides of the bowl and not mixing with the rest.

Now your date purée is a little cooler, add it to the mixture – this requires a bit of stirring now, so you might want to use a stand mixer if you have one. Oh, and get the oven heated to 180°C (400°F), with the fan on.

Slowly, add the flour, cornflour (cornstarch) and the other half of the baking powder to the date-y mixture. Continue stirring it until it's all mixed in.

Grease four small ramekins with butter, then pour in the mix.

Cook on the middle shelf of the oven for 50 minutes. If you're a real nerd and have a thermometer, you're looking for an internal temperature of 82°C (180°F).

While they're cooking, make your coffee sauce. Heat a saucepan over a medium heat and combine the brown sugar, butter and double (heavy) cream.

Once the butter and sugar have melted, let them boil for 30 seconds. You want all of the sugar crystals to dissolve.

Once dissolved, turn off the heat and stir in the espresso. Leave to cool if you're not eating it right away. You can even chill it and reheat it later if you need to hold on to it for a while – it'll last as long in the fridge as the cream was going to!

Once ready, carefully flip out of the ramekins, add the sauce, and you're done.

Grind Guide #028
Inventing Your Own Cocktails

So, your bar is fully stocked, loaded with equipment, and your friends are coming over – or at least you've arranged a harem of stuffed animals to be your drinking companions for the night. You've made the cocktails in this book, and perhaps others, but you want to mix something that really feels like it's yours.

How cocktails have evolved and developed is a subject for another book, but, simply put, there are several families of classics, and over the years people have been twisting them into new things. Occasionally, an entirely new family will emerge and, in turn, twists will be made on those.

Possibly the best example of a twist on a drink appears earlier in this book – the Tommy's Margarita (see p129), an unimaginatively named evolution of the classic Margarita. The most famous of the twists generally come with a good story, even if it's a bit of a myth. In this case Julio Bermejo, working at his parents' Mexican restaurant, swapped the orange liqueur used in the original for agave syrup. The restaurant was called Tommy's, hence the name.

Looking further back, the Margarita is itself a twist on a small family of drinks called 'daisies', in turn part of a larger family called 'sours', which you'll see on cocktail menus the world over. A sours formula is four parts spirit, two parts acid – typically lime or lemon – and one part sweet. If the sweetness in a sours is from a liqueur, the drink is a daisy – so a Margarita is technically a tequila daisy. As Julio Bermejo replaced the liqueur with agave syrup in his Tommy's Margarita, it's not a daisy, although it is descended from one. Keep up!

The daiquiri, another classic, is a rum sour. The Clover Club is a gin and raspberry sour, with the addition of egg white for foam. The infamous Pornstar Martini (see p135) is a vodka, vanilla and passion fruit sour. Making your own sours is fun and easy, but stay away from Google as you'll inevitably find out someone has beaten you to even the wildest of inventions, the bastards.

Almost every cocktail is a twist on another – so making something your own is as simple as finding a drink you like and making it better. Or sometimes worse. Let's take a look at your arsenal.

Spirits

You know them, you love them – except the occasional one you have bad memories of from university. We don't need to list these out for you, but the very basics are vodka, often made from potatoes; rum, made from molasses and sugar cane; whisky, from grain; tequila, from the agave plant; and, of course, gin, flavoured with juniper berries, but also quite literally anything. There are spirits beyond this, and spirits beyond those, but these are the headliners.

Liqueurs

Liqueurs are sweetened, flavoured alcohol – often weaker than spirits, at around 15 to 20 per cent ABV. In the bar, this is one of the ways we get flavours into drinks – you can think of coffee liqueurs, orange liqueurs, peach liqueurs, and lychee liqueurs as essentials. This is one of the easiest ways to start making your own twists on the classics.

Aperitivos

These are slightly cheating, as aperitivos are a more bitter Italian subset of liqueurs – you'll know them as Campari and Aperol. They're essentials, we're sure you'll agree.

Vermouths

Vermouths are wines that have been fortified and flavoured with botanicals. They're essential for Martinis, Manhattans, Negronis

and many others, and come in technicolour options, but you'll just need a sweet vermouth and a dry vermouth to get started.

Bitters

Bitters generally come in very small bottles, and you'll rarely add more than a drop to a drink. Angostura bitters are the quintessential bitters, and are used to make the Old Fashioned. Bitters are comparable to seasoning for drinks – a few dashes of a complementary bitters really adds complexity to a drink.

Sugar Syrup

Sugar syrups are, as you might imagine, mainly sweetness, but also sometimes flavour. Making basic sugar syrup is super easy – take equal parts sugar and hot water, dissolve, and chill. It will last in the fridge for a week. You can also buy syrups in hundreds of different flavours – these are the things you'll see people putting in their coffee, which isn't something a person should do.

Citrus

This needs no introduction, and plays a part in almost every cocktail. If you can, always juice your citrus fresh, and measure out your amounts. When you're working in cocktails, and not in the kitchen, Grind bartender Sam says the juice of one lemon is not a unit of measurement – but we'll show him. You'll also see orange juice and grapefruit juice in cocktails from time to time, but often these are more about adding sweetness.

On the next few pages, you'll find some drinks that are our very own. They've been invented according to these ideas, and we serve thousands of them every week across London.

Elderflower Spritz

Not quite a full classic, but certainly a Grind favourite for at least three seasons of the year. This is a great one for learning how to make cocktails, as it's got enough ingredients to enable you to play with the balance of the drink.

If you'd like to try the fancy cucumber twist garnish in the photo (see p148), make narrow slices lengthways on a cucumber with a sharp knife or a mandoline – but only if you promise to be careful. Then, roll the slice up, secure with a cocktail stick and place on top of the glass.

Makes 1
25ml (1fl oz) vodka
25ml (1fl oz) elderflower
  cordial
25ml (1fl oz) lemon juice
ice

50ml (2fl oz) prosecco
50ml (2fl oz) soda water
  (club soda)

Glass: wine glass
Garnish: cucumber

Pour the vodka, elderflower cordial and lemon juice into your glass. Give it all a good stir.

Fill your glass with ice, right up to the top, and then add your prosecco and soda.

Give it a quick final stir to chill everything, and then garnish with a thin slice of cucumber.

Vegan White Russian

As made famous by the Dude in 1998's *The Big Lebowski*, and made hot by us on page 127. Now, we're making it vegan – as it could have always been, really. We use oat cream, as it's our favourite and we believe it's the most sustainable and best-tasting alternative, but you can use anything you like. Pictured on p148.

Makes 1
20ml (¾fl oz) vodka
20ml (¾fl oz) Tia Maria
  – or other coffee
  liqueur
ice
100ml (4fl oz) oat cream
  – which you can pick
  up in most major
  supermarkets now

Glass: large latte glass
Garnish: cocoa powder
  (optional)

Pour the vodka and Tia Maria into the latte glass and mix.

Stack your glass with ice, right up to the brim.

Fill with your oat cream. You can garnish with a little cocoa powder, if that takes your fancy.

Skinny Colada

Yeah, we've no idea why this one's called Skinny. The regular Piña Colada isn't even that unhealthy, despite having the appearance of some sort of '70s dessert. Ours is a much shorter drink than the kind of thing you might be served on a cruise. We use a coconut rum, but you can just use a regular white rum as the coconut cream does the heavy lifting.

If you're looking for something longer, throw the whole lot into a blender with a frozen banana and blitz – although you'll need a bigger glass, of course. Pictured on p148–149.

Makes 1

50ml (2fl oz) white rum or coconut rum
50ml (2fl oz) pineapple juice
50ml (2fl oz) coconut cream

25ml (1fl oz) lime juice
ice

Glass: champagne coupe

Pour the whole lot into a shaker. Stack it up full of ice.

Shake it all up. You're looking for 15 seconds of good, vigorous shaking, so break a sweat.

Double strain – use both the strainer attachment and a fine strainer – into your glass.

Garnish if you like, and drink.

Pink Negroni

A Grind favourite. In a previous life it was called 'Millennial Pink', but we thought we'd better pay tribute to the classic that it's a twist on. This swaps a darker sweet vermouth for a lighter one, and adds peach and lemon juice. Pictured on p149.

Makes 1

25ml (1fl oz) Beefeater gin or other gin
25ml (1fl oz) Campari
25ml (1fl oz) Lillet Blanc vermouth

25ml (1fl oz) lemon juice
25ml (1fl oz) peach syrup
ice

Glass: clear rocks glass
Garnish: lemon slice

Pour all the ingredients into a shaker and fill it up to the top with ice. This one's nice and easy.

Shake it all up vigorously for 15 seconds.

Double strain – use both the strainer attachment and a fine strainer – into a rocks glass with fresh ice and add a slice of lemon for garnish.

Grind Guide #029
How to Survive Cooking Drunk

To cook drunk is to live dangerously. It's pretty safe to say that brunch as we know and love it stemmed from the prehistoric need for food and a lengthy debrief the morning after a big night out hunting bison or something – we don't know, we just made this up. But more recently another drunkenly prepared meal has manifested. We're talking about the post-evening-out snack, made late at night.

The sight of a group of people returning home to attempt to prepare food – in a kitchen full of loud, hot, sharp things that can hurt you – looks like the sort of thing that David Attenborough ought to be narrating. His dulcet tones will be lulling you into a sense of security, but you know that things are unlikely to end well for this badger cub. Like most things, there are a few secrets to the fine art of cooking drunk.

Stay Alive

Seriously, this one is important. We know nothing we could say could dissuade you from boiling water for pasta, but you should absolutely not be doing anything dangerous. We will allow you oven fries, but by no means should you even think about doing anything that involves hot oil. No pan frying, no deep frying. Butter knives and bread knives are acceptable, and that's it – no meat cleavers, no chef's knives. If you even think about a mandoline, you'll get what's coming to you. We'd also like to hope that you don't decide 2am is the moment to work on your julienne carrots.

The Playlist

While the safest choice here is, as always, a playlist of absolute belters, you're rarely more than a few shuffles away from something that's going to make you cry. Whitney Houston, okay, but find yourself in 1989-era Taylor Swift and you're going to embarrass yourself. I have seen the greatest minds of my generation destroyed by Demi Lovato's 'Skyscraper'.

Keep It Down

No, obviously not the music – we're talking about not redecorating your bathroom with your stomach contents in five to ten minutes' time. This generally comes down to the food you're choosing. There is a time in your life for seafood, and it is not this. Nothing with an icky texture, either.

Honourable mentions here go to carbohydrates: bread, pasta and potatoes, in literally any form and combination.

Take Your Time

Look, you're hardly in the best state of mind while doing it – and you're probably hungry in a way only drunk people are – but drunk cooking should be a labour of love. If you're doing things right, by which we mean terribly, it'll mysteriously take forever.

Grind Guide #030
A Good Night's Sleep

As much as we trade it for a good time, a good night's sleep is really important. It's hard to lose sleep for any period without feeling its effects on your mental and physical health. There'll always be times where sleep comes second – when you don't want the best night ever to end or you're trying to finish the book you've been writing for months – but the rest of the while it should be top of your list. It's just good self-care (see p100).

Like anything worthwhile, getting a good night's sleep requires a little preparation. We've tried and tested some tips here – which is more than we can say for most of our advice – and having done this nightly for some time now, it's safe to say we're experts in the field.

The Three-Hour Rule

While we'd love a siesta to be part of everyday life, unfortunately we haven't even managed to take so much as a lunch break in years. At this point, it's move to the continent or give up on that dream entirely. While there's nothing better than a nap on a Sunday afternoon after a roast, if you want a chance of getting a decent night's sleep, then don't eat dinner at 11pm. From our extensive research, over decades, we've found that eating at least three hours before you head to bed gives your body enough time to do whatever it does. We're not sure of the science behind this, but it's something to do with being vertical.

Cleanliness Is Close to Godliness

So, maybe this is just us, but we think getting into your bed without having a shower or a bath first is disgusting and not something a human being should do – it's more like something a rat or dog would do. Your bed should be a place of comfort, and there's nothing less comforting than carrying around the days' assorted smells with you – whether other people's or your own. There's also some actual science here – something about raising your body temperature improving your sleep quality. It doesn't have to be a long leisurely soak, but you can't go wrong with a bubble bath – treat yourself.

Step Away from the Screen

Yes, really. We've all heard about the blue light–yellow light thing. We're talking TVs, iPhones, tablets, laptops and anything else that gives off that lovely glow. While there's science behind it in the way your body is programmed to react to light – the baby lizard inside you thinks it's the sun – there's also a lot to be said for just taking some time to wind down, tune out, and just be with yourself or your bed companion. A lot of people swear by keeping their devices out of the bedroom entirely, but that's probably more a temptation thing. What we do know is that the little rituals you're used to doing before bed keep your mind in check. Sweet dreams.

Index

Acknowledgements

It probably reflects very poorly on me that I have to thank so many people for their perseverance in making this book a reality. Perhaps most of all, my agent Charlotte Lake, who managed to create an entire human being in the time since she and I first discussed writing a book in 2018.

More recently, I'm deeply grateful to have been able to work with Sarah Lavelle and the team at Quadrille. Special thanks to Stacey Cleworth and Alicia House for – again – their patience and perseverance.

Closer to home, I'll offer my begrudging gratitude to David Abrahamovitch, co-founder and CEO of Grind, for letting me write a book that was this self-indulgent.

Of course, none of this would have been possible without contributors from Grind in many shapes and sizes; Kyle Boyce, Frankie Cooke, Jaz Dye, Howard Gill, Emma Ralph, Antonia Roberts and Sam Trevethyen.

I wrote this book for a lot of reasons, but mostly to stop myself from feeling lonely, at a point in my life when I felt most alone. I'm grateful for Alex, as well as Alice, Luke and Matt, for making me feel much less so.

Our lawyers assure me that this is a work of fiction and that all characters, businesses, events and incidents – no matter how curiously familiar – are the product of my imagination.

Some names have been changed out of spite. Others have been left in – again, mostly out of spite. Any resemblance to actual persons, living or dead, should at least appear to be coincidental.

Publishing Director Sarah Lavelle
Editor Stacey Cleworth
Head of Design Claire Rochford
Photographer Luke Albert
Food Stylist Libby Silbermann
Prop Stylist Charlie Phillips
Head of Production Stephen Lang
Production Controller Nikolaus Ginelli

Author Teddy Robinson
Contributors Kyle Boyce, Frankie Cooke, Jaz Dye, Emma Ralph, Antonia Roberts, Sam Trevethyen
Photography contributors Handover, Andy Donohoe, Teddy Robinson, David Sheldrick, Richard Heald

Published in 2021 by Quadrille, an imprint of Hardie Grant Publishing

52–54 Southwark Street
London SE1 1UN
quadrille.com

Cataloguing in Publication Data: a catalogue record for this book is available from The British Library.

Text © Grind Holdings Ltd 2021
All Photography © Luke Albert, except for:
Pages 6, 10, 56, 60–1, 64, 78, 79, 120 and 136 Handover;
9 Andy Donohoe; 39, 43 Teddy Robinson; 46 David Sheldrick; 114 Richard Heald. All © Grind Holdings Ltd 2021.
Design © Quadrille 2021

ISBN 978 1 78713 708 0
Printed in China

MIX
Paper from responsible sources
FSC™ C020056
FSC
www.fsc.org